BREAKING FREE

BREAKING FREE

DAVID HALL

OM Publishing
Bromley, Kent

British Library Cataloguing in Publication Data

Hall, David
  Breaking free.
  1. Christianity. Conversion of non-
  Christians. Personal observations—
  Collections
  I. Title
  248.2'46'0922

STL ISBN 1–85078–037–4

STL Books are published by Send The Light
(Operation Mobilisation), PO Box 48, Bromley, Kent,
England, BR1 3JH

Production and Printing in England by
Nuprint Ltd, Station Road, Harpenden, Herts, AL5 4SE.

Contents

Thanks . . .

When I was asked to write *Breaking Free* towards the end of last year I did not fully anticipate the excitement and encouragement it would give me as I investigated some of the dramatic stories.

My own involvement was at the invitation of Dave Brown and Steve Chilcraft—I owe them thanks for even thinking of me. But the book would not have been possible without the involvement of Operation Mobilisation workers across Europe and in particular a number of people who have given much of their time and enthusiasm.

To Marcel, in Czechoslovakia; Christine, in Vienna; Linda, in Paris; and Oriana in Zurich; my grateful thanks for spending hours interpreting.

To Andy whose house I used in Vienna; Harvey and Jenny in Bremen; the staff at Best Hope in Switzerland and at Capernwray in Lancashire, England; all those who made my travel and arrangements so smooth and comfortable.

To those individuals whose stories are featured—

for their time, the willingness to recall often trau-matic events in their lives so that others could be enriched, and to their families who provided hos-pitality. My own Christian pathway seems so straightforward and uncomplicated alongside their journeys of faith.

And to Colin Edwards—the minister who led me to the Lord Jesus Christ.

To these good people, thank you.

I

Europe: Love's battlefield

Europe is enjoying the longest period of peace since Christmas Day 800 AD, when Charlemagne was crowned Holy Roman Emperor to bring Europe into being. But physical peace has brought with it moral frustration and spiritual unrest. Peace of heart for the individual seems harder to find than national peace.

The memories of two world wars are gradually dimming, and with them go the established record that the smallest of the five continents has also been one of the most adventurous, innovative and inquisitive.

For a history of discovery in world travel, science and medicine, is behind Europe, and it now struggles to evade the shackles of the Eastern bloc on one flank and the feeling of being used by the Americans in the West.

And with those frustrating juggling acts there are newer legacies of progress: massive unemployment, breakdown in family life, the loss of historic moral values, an erosion of law and order, and greater vulnerability to lawless minorities.

While the dominance of the dollar is disintegrating and the icy-coldness of the USSR is melting slightly, Europe faces fresh challenges of an economic nature from the Far East as Japan, Taiwan, South Korea and China make their own microchip invasions.

Plastic cards, more leisure, and the amazingly successful take-over by mass-communication techniques have all contributed to the most radical alteration in life-styles in the history of the continent.

Politically the European Economic Community has attempted to draw some of the continental countries together beginning with the six founder nations; France, Belgium, Germany, Italy, Luxembourg and the Netherlands. Three more joined in 1973—Denmark, Ireland and the United Kingdom—and Greece became the tenth member in 1981. Portugal and Spain joined the club five years later. But if it has brought benefits of transport and ease of cross-border movement it has also introduced the indecency of food mountains, an annual argument over farming and fishing protection and financial frustrations for its 320 million citizens; troubles that are also not remote for the remainder of Europe's 820 million inhabitants.

Immigration adds to the problems facing European countries as millions flock to the West for a new life. Calls for massive increased aid to the Third World and the escalating pressures of providing enough work for its own population, make their mark on the European scene.

And if governments find it difficult to plan adequately and generate economic growth and stability, the increasing pressures on individuals are causing a deeper malaise. The frantic speed of life, demands in business for results, frustrations of getting and keeping a job, the fragmenting of family life as families move further apart and couples more readily accept the divorce option or decide to separate, and the resulting legacy of one-parent families or deserted children drives huge wedges into the social fabric of society, hacking away the foundations which once stabilised nations. For while individuals of many nations claim a desire to uphold the institution of marriage they also want a far greater degree of sexual freedom, the very thing which threatens a couple's personal love.

There is still much that is good in Europe—artistically and socially—but too often it becomes simply something to cling to, a memory of a long-gone existence.

Instead Europeans have lost the ability to face life. Indeed the European Values Survey 1981 shows that they are an anxious people—twenty-one per cent of Belgians admitted to feeling anxious often, nineteen per cent of the French, and seventeen per cent of the Italians questioned also said they felt anxious 'often'. West Germans and Danes were much less prone to anxiety, with the British, Irish and Dutch significantly more happy and relaxed. But the West Germans were more aggressive.

All need something extra out of life. Living just isn't enough. There are, however, thousands in Europe who have discovered what that missing ingredient to life is and have had their lives transformed in the discovery. That is what this book is about. For while industry, commerce and unemployment can merely add frustrations to life it *is* possible to feel free, experience peace and tranquillity despite the enormous pressures of life at the close of the twentieth century—the fastest-moving, most cataclysmic century in the world's history.

This book is the story of nine people from different backgrounds who have made that discovery. From backgrounds which include the bustle of inner-city life, poor family backgrounds, aggressive youth, searching minds, broken marriages, desperate illness, wandering immigrants, Communism, they have each plotted a very different pathway but had the same life-changing meeting. They met Jesus Christ, the Son of God. And from then on their lives were very different. The problems didn't always go away; they still had to live life with all its complex dilemmas. The difference was that after that meeting not only were they different people with different outlooks but they had a friend who could help. For those whose stories follow are individuals who have had that life-changing power given to them and accepted all that it meant. It has been a personal privilege and pleasure to meet them and learn of their histories.

For some, like Pavel in Eastern Europe, it is frustratingly difficult to follow the author of that faith—Jesus Christ—but despite the rigorous deterrent of a State which has atheism at its very heart he, and thousands of other Christians, manage to thrive and grow. In the cosy comfort of the minister's study above a church it was impossible not to admire Pavel's staunch new-found stability. His name, incidentally, has had to be changed to protect not simply himself but others in that country from persecution.

In the more affluent countries where the gods of wealth, influence, personal possessions and even mystic religions reign supreme, individuals still manage to discover that Jesus Christ presents them with a more perfect pattern of living, one which defies national trends and accomplishments.

In some of Europe's capitals I have met people whose backgrounds make it seem like a miracle that they could have come into contact with Christianity at all—much less become part of it. My lifetime in journalism has enabled me to select nine stories from thousands of possibilities. I have not looked for particularly sensational personalities, but lives which, somewhere along the line, might be following the pattern of your own. These people looked for satisfaction and fulfilment in life in a variety of different ways. They were basically ordinary people living with the frustrations of a modern world.

You will read about men and women who discovered God in the hustle of inner-city life; in the search for moral absolutes; as they felt the bitter dissatisfaction of sexual, and even theological, life-styles.

Their experience, and the experience of countless thousands of other Europeans, is that the one thing that could bring stability and ultimate peace to individuals is Christianity. Taken to Greece on the Continent's eastern edge by Saint Paul himself when Christianity was in its infancy, it has managed to survive the ravages of two thousand years and still commands respect. At the centre of the struggles for better working conditions, greater equality, a fairer apportionment of wealth, have often been Christians whose sense of devotion to moral causes has led them to inspire many of the fights for improvement seen over the centuries.

But even more important than that has been the radical alteration it has brought in the lives of individuals. Christianity professes to be a radical re-think of living conditions and understanding.

It can change your life. In fact God wants to change your life. Read how God still loves Europe and Europeans—including you . . .

2

Bjørn: A new heart

Beep! Beep! The small black machine clipped to the pocket of Bjørn Kristiansen's shirt pocket came alive. He moved his short, sturdy frame towards the telephone in the small office alongside the bedroom of his home and dialled a number. As the immediate response was made his comments brought the answer for which he had been waiting for 105 days. 'Fantastic,' he called out.

Downstairs his wife, Ann, had heard the noise and waited for the news. As Bjørn called to her she made for the corner where a suitcase had been standing for the same number of days. While she was putting it ready by the door she heard Bjørn telephone a taxi, give his name and the reason for the call. He rested the telephone in its cradle; they both knew that he was now only hours away from the most serious operation he had ever faced.

Bjørn was to have a new heart. The years of living with the knowledge that his heart was increasingly getting worse had led to this occasion: a heart transplant.

Ann, at five foot six inches tall, the same height as her husband, looked up as he descended the stairs and entered the room. His face showed the excitement he felt. They walked from the house, Bjørn squeezing into the rear seat while Ann closed the front door of their house in Oslo, strode down the path and joined her husband. They both knew that within an hour of the bleep Bjørn must be undergoing preparation for surgery.

Inside the hospital Bjørn looked at Ann. He smiled, in the confident way she had come to expect of him, and spoke. 'It is strange to think that the Valley of the Shadow of Death is here in Rikshospitalet, but the Lord is with me.' As the words left his lips she could almost see the thoughts going through his mind. There was a time when such confidence would have been placed in a very different direction, when the name of God would not have come from those lips, for Bjørn Kristiansen, who was about to be given a new heart, had had the heart transplant he had really wanted twenty years previously—and that one had been far more important than he could ever hope the imminent surgery would be . . .

Born in May 1934 in Oslo, Bjørn began life in the Ila district; his father, a military musician, played the trombone, among other instruments, in the army and when his division moved to Halden near the Swedish border the family moved too. Bjørn soon found life had some puzzles for him. One of the mysteries he discovered came when a newfound friend took him one Sunday to the Sunday school run by the local Salvation Army citadel, but despite his enjoyment and desire to return he was banned by his parents. Religion was not a family way of life.

Then, on 5 April 1940, Nazi Germany invaded Norway. Vidkun Quisling who, despite only getting a two per cent majority in the previous Parliamentary elections, had voted himself Prime Minister, set up a government in collaboration with the Nazi leaders to give the world the word for such a traitor—Quisling. And worse was to come: Bjørn's father was taken away along with thirty-five thousand Norwegians—many gifted musicians and teachers—and released after a day while many others were kept in a concentration camp.

As the family returned to Oslo in February 1942 schools were closed, moving into homes, and Bjørn sat for hours in the local library reading. Every book in the child's section was known to him during those months until the end of the war in May 1945 as he began a lifelong obsession of reading and enjoying literature. At eleven he became the child with a key round his neck—the loop of string on which it hung being his link with the family home while his mother was working all day.

The lone experience at Sunday school was a dim memory when Bjørn, as a young man, became interested in the Communist movement and enthusiastically studied Karl Marx and Lenin. They promised a new future and great ideals—until later, as a sailor, he visited Russian ports and saw the conditions of the peasants and the quick turnover of political leaders. Bjørn idolised his sports teacher, an athletic man who also taught religious education. It was this teacher who bred the thought in Bjørn's mind that was to taint much of his religious thinking: 'The Bible is simply a book of Jewish myths,' the teacher explained to his class and many, like Bjørn, listened and believed.

If life at home and school lacked the excitement the studious young man dreamed of, he very soon moved in a direction to find more thrills.

At sixteen he joined the Fred Olsen line as a sailor and went to Brazil, sailing along the coast on a cargo ship doing the menial tasks that were expected of a young rating but doing them briskly and picking up a feeling for the sea. The sea became his life—and Bjørn was determined to beat not only the waves which he occasionally saw towering above and about the vessels on which he sailed, but the system that determined how sailors made it to the top positions within the company.

He studied, worked and sailed—all the while moving towards his goal of excellence.

'I know the way to the top,' he confided in a friend. 'You stand on the hands of those beneath you on the ladder—and lick the boots of those above you.'

It worked. And as he soared higher his life took on a sharp edge; drinking, swearing, and rejecting anything he couldn't immediately understand.

Sitting in a pub in Oslo on one occasion he watched as a young enthusiastic street-preacher entered and announced: 'Jesus is coming soon.' They were the only words the young man was allowed to say as Bjørn grabbed his collar and propelled him through the doors into the street. Religion wasn't one of the things he had time for.

For Bjørn Kristiansen—despite his name—God didn't exist. But there were occasions that he couldn't explain when he began to doubt. Each time he raised the brass sextant to his eyes to read the position of the stars and plot the position of his ship on the ocean with no land mass for miles, he puzzled over who had made the heavens in such a perfect way; 'there must be a creator,' he mused.

And one day in southern Norway when he was concentrating on navigational studies in a marine school he suddenly felt that God was real and talking to him—it was as if the voice came through a long pipe—and he spoke back.

On a later incident he was in Jamaica and his shore visit was delayed because of extra duties. When he finally made his way across the gangplank to the land he could hear noise coming from a clump of trees. It must be a pub, he considered, and made his way towards the noise, slipping into the last wooden chair, watching and listening as people clapped and sang before he realised it was a group of black Pentecostal Christians. Perhaps it was the similarity to jazz that attracted him? He stayed and listened as a white-haired preacher spoke aggressively about God and talked of God's Son Jesus Christ. He called for anyone who wanted a new life to go to the front, but Bjørn was rooted to his seat. Afterwards the preacher shook his hand and put the question bluntly to the young man: 'Wouldn't you like to be a Christian?'

Deep down the young officer felt he would, but the setting was too exotic; the temptation had to be avoided at least until he had returned to Norway and could consider it more carefully. It was to be several years before he thought about it again.

Soon he had made it to the top in his chosen profession. Officer examinations at the highly acclaimed Norwegian School of Seamanship, which overlooked the city's harbour complex, were soon a thing of the past. He had moved through the ranks past third and second officer, to first and then to captain—at twenty-seven, top of his class, the best student with ninety-eight points and one of the youngest men in Norway ever to hold a captain's certificate. But it wasn't enough, he insisted on taking his extra master's exams and becoming a highly qualified navigational officer, able to teach the mysteries of guidance at sea.

The love of music which his father had instilled in him wasn't forgotten either. Bjørn mastered a five-string banjo and helped form a traditional jazz band, the Hot Saints, which was to become one of the country's leading groups. They played all over Norway and Bjørn added lecturing in jazz to his accomplishments as he travelled. His deep love was traditional jazz and when he had the opportunity to tour New Orleans he jumped at the chance of visiting the district which gave birth to the sound he loved. He played alongside George Lewis and met the king of jazz, Louis Armstrong himself. There was little in life that Bjørn didn't get if he wanted it enough.

He was an expert on traditional jazz and considered himself a skilled hand too at drinking, lying, swearing and tough living. Religion was relegated to the few religious records on board ship which the sailors occasionally called out to be played for a laugh. Despite an empty feeling inside Bjørn was, to outside eyes, a very successful man.

As one of the country's youngest captains he was seconded to the United Nations in Indonesia to train local sailors in coastal transport, to enable them to deliver oil among the thirteen thousand islands in the group. When the UN contract was over he stayed among the islands he had come to love, working for the state-operated oil company Pertamina.

The importance of the key job made Bjørn even more self-reliant and self-important. He needed no one else.

It was a feeling of breathlessness that first provided the clue that something was wrong physically; a clue the 28-year-old ignored until he suddenly found himself lying prone on the top of the stairs during a visit to his home—he had passed out for no apparent reason and couldn't remember why. Breathlessness and fainting were the prelude to an operation to split a valve in his heart, an aortic valvotomy. He returned to Indonesia after successful surgery and couldn't believe it four years later when a doctor warned of further heart trouble. In previous weeks he had noticed his legs were becoming swollen—it was diagnosed as a serious oedema in both legs—they had collected water because of the poor condition of his heart. He was flown to the Rikshospitalet in Oslo for emergency treatment. First doctors inserted tubes into his legs to drain off the excess fluid, taking off an extraordinary thirteen litres.

Then he was told he was in line for heart surgery; the aortic valve in his heart was not working correctly—he needed an artificial replacement. For twelve months the medical officers monitored his progress until they considered he was fit enough to face the operation. During that time there were occasions when he appeared to be regaining his strength—and times of distressing sickness.

But in August the following year, 1967, his condition worsened: fluid on the lungs—often the last stages of his particular ailment—struck with the threat that he would drown in the fluids produced by his own body.

He was rushed into the operating theatre, his lungs punctured and the fluid drained. His mother gave permission for an emergency operation and the surgeons began the delicate task of replacing his damaged aortic valve with an artificial one of plastic and steel. What is now a common operation was then still very much in its infancy.

He was wheeled unconscious into the intensive care ward with nurses constantly monitoring his progress, looking for signs of stability and recovery. As Bjørn lay unconscious he could sense himself rising out of the darkness, but wanted to sink back into the depths of forgetfulness.

Regularly the medical staff tested their patient, checking for life to make sure that he was not 'brain dead'—merely existing by the modern miracle of the heart machine and the drip tubes which pulsated life and food into his veins. Several weeks after the operation, in the middle of October, an elderly nurse, Sister Olga, had carefully clipped the rubber suction pads of an electro-encephalogram to Bjørn's head to carry out a brain test when his eyes flickered open. He was alive and responding. He heard the voice of the nurse gently whispering into his ear . . . 'You are very ill, be careful. You could die, but Jesus Christ loves you very much—he died for you on the cross. If you put your trust in him, he will give you eternal life whatever happens here.'

As her patient's flickering eyes betrayed interest, she quoted from the Bible: Jesus said, 'I am the resurrection and the life. He who believes in me will live, even though he dies; and whoever lives and believes in me will never die.' (John 11:25-26, New International Version).

The tough sea-captain stared up through misty eyes thinking what a brave woman she was for daring to speak to him in that way. He sensed the concern she had for him; the first time anyone had ever spoken to him personally about God. He hoped she would say no more. But she added: 'I will pray for you.'

As Bjørn clenched his lips round the pipe that searched its way into his chest, sucking away the dangerous fluids, unable to speak, he thought it was enough. He nodded his agreement—prayer, after all, was just a word. The sister bowed her head, gripped his hand in hers and started to talk to a God he had only sensed in lightning flashes previously. 'Lord, you can see this man lying sick on this bed . . . will you save him? . . . help him to love you and give himself to you.'

Looking at Bjørn she smiled and told him: 'You must pray too. Inside.'

For twelve months Bjørn had lain on the hospital bed gradually feeling more desperate and lonely. The friends who had visited him regularly at first had not been for months; only his close family now came to see him. Two months before, when he had been visited by the anaesthetist before the operation, he had watched the summer leaves dancing patterns against the windows of his ward. Now there were only bare branches as the last autumn leaves fluttered to earth. He had lost the summer— but he didn't intend to lose anything else, especially something so precious as the feeling that was coming over him as the sister spoke and prayed. In his heart he cried out: 'Lord, if you are there reveal yourself to me. I want to know you in reality, just as this nurse knows you. I don't know what it all means, but I know I need you.'

When the doctors made their ward visit later that day they could not believe the transformation. Gently easing the tubes from his mouth and the intravenous tubes from their positions taped to his arms, the doctor asked Bjørn: 'You look better— would you like anything to eat?'

It had been weeks since Bjørn had eaten and he mumbled, 'Rice and chicken. I would like some rice and chicken.' The years of Indonesian living had made their mark.

Within minutes, it seemed, an orderly was standing alongside the bed helping him into a sitting position and carrying a small tray containing a dish with rice and carefully chopped pieces of chicken. Without even questioning the arrival of so unusual a dish in a Norwegian hospital, Bjørn spooned the small amount into his mouth, savouring each particle with the relish known only to a man who had not eaten proper food for months.

The removal of the drip tubes left him free to turn his body onto its side—again something he had been unable to do. Bliss! He didn't then know just how ill he had been. His sister-in-law, Margit, had sat by the edge of the bed just days before, knowing that medically he was near to death. Now he was on the road to recovery. The next day it took a couple of nurses to restrain his over-enthusiasm as they caught him dangling his legs over the edge of the bed in an attempt to walk to the toilet unaided.

Each day he got stronger. Four days after the nurse's prayer he was perched on the edge of the bed when his nephew called to visit. The nephew, thinking Bjørn was still desperately ill, pushed open the doors to the ward and saw the figure sitting up. He screamed, dropped the bag he was carrying and rushed to the ward sister's office thinking Bjørn had died and a stranger was in his bed. As he sat and talked, when realisation dawned, he could not believe the transformation.

It was only days before Bjørn was transferred from intensive care to a medical ward with the extra freedom this gave him. Depression, however, had set in. He had asked his mother to bring him a Bible and, despite her scepticism—'you're better now, you don't need a Bible!'—she had done so. When he stared at it, all he could see were black squiggles . . . the two months of unconsciousness had made their mark and it would be a few days before his brain cleared sufficiently to send the correct messages to his eyes to enable him to read clearly.

The depression deepened. Four days after his recovery it gripped Bjørn so much that he felt he would burst; he was fully aware that Jesus Christ had touched his life and done something miraculous, but he was conscious of the many times in the past when he had done wrong things—his drinking, swearing, lying and cheating preyed on his mind. Convicted, he felt he had to do something.

On the evening of 18 October 1967 he recalled a brass plaque on the wall of a mission house in Oslo he had passed many times on his way to the docks: 'If you have spiritual problems come and talk with us,' it read. Bjørn looked around and ensured there were no nurses watching, grabbed his clothes from the wardrobe alongside his bed, dressed and walked out of the front door of the hospital, desperately trying not to show how unsteady he was on his feet, and took a taxi outside the main gate.

At the mission he tapped on the door and waited. The door was opened by a middle-aged man wearing a pair of slacks and pullover—unlike any minister Bjørn had ever seen. 'Can I help you?' he asked.

'I have run away from the hospital. I must talk to you about Jesus Christ,' Bjørn blurted out.

'I have been a seamen's pastor, I know your type—in and out, always in a hurry,' smiled the minister, inviting Bjørn inside.

In the snug comfort of a homely study the minister, Hans Christian Lier, first picked up the telephone. 'I must call the hospital to let them know you are all right,' he explained. Bjørn could hear the surprised voice at the other end of the line. The sister had been searching the hospital for him and had just sent nurses out of the building to see whether he had thrown himself from the window— she knew he was worried and depressed. Even though he was not holding the phone he could sense her relief.

As the minister spoke, quietly and calmly, Bjørn realised he could stay. The minister had promised to ensure he returned to the hospital later that evening. Hans Christian Lier leaned back in his chair as Bjørn poured out his story. He recalled his past and then told of his operation and his surprise at waking and being prayed for by the sister. He recounted his amazement at the feeling that God was going to help him, and the depression that had overwhelmed him as he considered his past. He paused for breath.

'Is that all?'

'No, I've only just begun,' continued Bjørn.

'Well, stop for a minute and let me speak,' the minister interrupted. 'I'll tell you what God wants you to know.'

Taking a well-worn Bible from its place on the study table the pastor edged his chair alongside Bjørn's and began to show him sections. Rapidly flicking through the pages he read of the birth of Jesus Christ and then his death. He spoke of the reason for the death—'Because men are sinners and nothing unholy can enter the presence of God they need a sacrifice—something to take the place of their sin. In the old days they used to kill a lamb but God wanted to introduce one sacrifice that would end that for good. He sent his only Son, Jesus Christ, who was sacrificed on behalf of everyone who calls on him and accepts the power of his death. Three days after he died and was buried in a tomb Jesus rose from the dead and went to sit alongside his Father in heaven, reigning supreme over the world to which he had demonstrated his love. You need to believe on Jesus and take him into your own life; you need to ask him to take away all your sins, and he will. And not just take them away—but they will be completely forgotten.

'If you mention your past sins to Jesus he will say, "Bjørn, what are you talking about?" They will be forgotten.'

After two months in a coma Bjørn knew what forgetfulness was . . . his mind flickered back just a few hours to when he was looking for his spectacles and then saw them on the bedside table where he had put them minutes before. Other instances of memory loss came to him. That sort of forgetfulness on God's part made the offer of a new life even better. God, he realised, was willing to give him that new start and forget his past.

'I want you to read this passage,' the minister continued, passing over his Bible and pointing to the beginning of a section. Bjørn read of how a man named Matthew was called by Jesus and gave up his job to follow him. 'Now read it again and put your own name in place of the name Matthew,' the minister instructed.

Bjørn did so: 'As Jesus went on from there, he saw a man named Bjørn Kristiansen sitting at the tax collector's booth. "Follow me," he told him, and Bjørn Kristiansen got up and followed him . . .'

'The tax collector's booth is like this world . . . you are sitting in the world waiting, and Jesus has come and called you.'

'But how can I follow a person who died two thousand years ago?'

'Because Jesus is alive—he rose from the dead—and because he is alive he has the power to offer you eternal life. What did Matthew do when Jesus called him?'

'"He got up and followed . . ."' Bjørn read.

'That's what you have to do. Make a decision. Decide to follow Jesus.'

Bjørn bowed his head, and the minister prayed. After a short prayer he told Bjørn to ask Jesus to come into his life and change him, to give him new life; in a halting prayer the sea-captain, more used to lording it over the men under his control, bowed before the minister and before God, and did so.

As relief, happiness, excitement and new life bubbled around inside him, Bjørn knew that something miraculous had happened. He grasped the minister's hand, thanking him, and refused the offer of a lift back to the hospital, preferring to walk. As he did so he walked carefully, not because of his delicate health but because all along the route he was conscious that Jesus was beside him at last, and he felt the presence so real he couldn't help but make a passage for two people between the late-night pedestrians.

At the hospital the sister jovially ticked him off, noticing at the same time the radical change that had come over the patient she had seen near to death just days before.

And Bjørn couldn't help but notice the smiling eyes and greetings from other nurses as they walked past his bed. What he didn't know was that a number of the Christian nurses in the hospital had been pacing outside the intensive care ward in which he had spent those dangerous months, praying for his salvation. Their prayers had been answered.

The next day the doctor gave Bjørn his daily check and scribbled on his medical chart. The previous day had the verdict, 'The patient is in a

state of depression.' This time he held the clip-
board, looked at Bjørn, smiled and wrote, 'Today
the patient is very elated.'

A week later Bjørn was discharged. But the man
who walked from Oslo's Rikshospitalet was a very
different man from the one flown from Indonesia
twelve months before. Not only had he regained his
health but he knew that inside him something had
changed: he really was a new creature in Jesus
Christ as the Bible promised.

He went to the jazz club and told them of his
decision to be a Christian. The change in their
former partner was evident and one of the group
called out: 'It's either Jesus or us. You'd better
choose . . . we don't want you to be our bad con-
science.' Bjørn chose Christ—and lost his friends.

The local church didn't treat him much better.
When he spoke to the priest he was told, 'Come
back in a month—we have a meeting then for men.'
It wasn't enough for the new-born Christian. He
wanted to meet other Christians immediately.

Back at sea he discovered the love of alcohol had
gone and within days his ship-mates were asking
him what had happened. 'You don't swear any
more,' they said in puzzlement.

Bjørn felt he had been given a new life 'in a
double sense': one physically, but more important,
spiritually. He began to notice how much better life
was as a Christian. 'I don't have to lie any more,' he
told a friend. 'Before I often forgot what stories I
had told different people—now I simply tell the
truth and life is easier.'

Visiting Hong Kong to investigate the possibility
of working from there he felt a sudden surge of pain

in his chest as he was crossing the road. He staggered into a hotel alongside the road with the help of a doorman. Almost as soon as he had been laid in a chair in the foyer a kind face was peering at him, hands gently feeling his pulse. He felt the slight prick of a needle in his arm, and the pain began to leave him. Hong Kong's only heart specialist was staying at the hotel and had responded to the call from the management to help Bjørn, saving his life. Later investigation showed Bjørn also had hepatitis, so he returned to Norway for more tests and treatment.

During the six weeks he was in hospital recuperating he was visited by representatives of a Christian seamen's group—the Brotherhood of the Sea—who helped him. Ironically his mother, who had put up with him singing his way into the house drunk on many occasions, later refused to allow him to live there as a Christian, so he was forced to pack his bags and look for somewhere to stay. Even as he was completing the packing, however, he had a phone call from a friend who had got to go to hospital for a few weeks and wondered if Bjørn would look after his flat for a time—it was ideal accommodation until he returned once again to Indonesia.

This time he returned to work with Pertamina as a trouble-shooter. Based in Semerang he spent his time being taken to different islands to sort out a variety of problems.

It was one of his regular visits to the local hospital for the check-up, which he knew was important, which introduced him to the next person who would help fashion his new life. As he wriggled on

the hard wooden bench in the waiting room he
noticed an elderly Chinese man reading a black
book. Bjørn edged over to him. 'Excuse me, is that a
Bible?'

The man replied in the affirmative and Bjørn told
him, 'I'm a Christian too!' The astute Chinese man,
however, began to sense the newness of Bjørn's
faith and invited the Norwegian to his house for a
Bible study. Bjørn became a regular visitor to the
Chinese home, soaking up the Bible teaching like a
sponge dropped into a bowl of water. His brain,
honed on years of study and reading, grasped at the
different facets of the faith and understood them as
he began to attend the local church and developed a
thirst for the Bible. He loved the Indonesian church
and the dynamic, adventurous Christianity he saw
all around him as Indonesia experienced the
scorching heat of revival fires.

'Why do you live in the mountains—come and live
with us!' invited his Chinese friend and Bjørn did,
moving into a small house alongside and eating his
meals in the small home of his friend. His Christian
life expanded as he saw the way the Indonesians
were changed by the gospel. Young people toured
the islands preaching and talking about their faith.
Hundreds became Christians. Bjørn met a man
who had been running a cinema until he was converted to Christianity. When the cinema opened its
doors the following day it was as a church! A
tobacco-seller accepted Christ into his life and
became a taxi-driver. Bjørn saw men changed as
radically as he had been.

He began to help reach outlying islands by radio,
learning the Indonesian language and using his

regular trips to Singapore and his own money as the means of buying spare parts for the radio station—parts unobtainable without his help. A new desire began to burn in Bjørn's heart as he listened to the radio messages and saw the effects of the Christian message: he knew the thirteen thousand islands better than anyone, he had sailed round and between them for years. What was needed was a ship equipped to visit all the islands with the gospel.

The dream began to grip him until eventually he gave up his job and returned to Oslo, taking work as a claims adjuster for a shipping company, while he looked for a suitable vessel. In London, England, he visited Lloyds, the world-renowned shipping offices, and was invited to meet members of the Christian Union attached to the office. As he chatted with other Christians and shared his vision they told him of a similar dream by a group named Operation Mobilisation, who wanted such a ship not simply to visit Indonesia but ports all over the world! Bjørn was amazed. He wrote to OM and met with leaders at the European headquarters in Belgium to discuss the project.

He discovered that for six years they had been praying that sailors would be converted, and for a ship that would have a world-wide ministry. Bjørn had become a Christian during that time—an answer to their prayers—and now he agreed to work with them. It was he, in fact, who showed a letter about the project to a Norwegian ship-broker and a week later OM was offered the derelict and dilapidated ship the MV *Umanak*, named after a mountain in Greenland. Bjørn persuaded OM leaders to inspect the vessel in a Copenhagen dock and later knelt on the quayside with the mission's founder George Verwer, praying that if God wanted them to have the ship no one else would get it. The boat that had once been a Royal Danish passenger and cargo ship, sailing between Denmark and Greenland, became theirs!

Bjørn became the first captain on the newly named MV *Logos* vessel, proudly manning the bridge as it was towed from Copenhagen to Rotterdam to be repaired and refitted for its new task afloat. For two years he was its skipper they included two trips to Indonesia, visits rich in spiritual rewards. Captain Kristiansen, in his peaked cap and dark uniform, with the four bars of gold braid round his wrist topped by a golden diamond, was soon a welcome visitor to many ports in Asia. He was part of the floating mission and a hundred and thirty-nine young Christians from over twenty lands. The Christian message hit home with precision as they worked together with local Christians, churches and missionaries.

On board Bjørn met Ann, a former nurse now working on *Logos* after some years in the OM offices in Austria and Belgium. They were later married in Oslo, the service being conducted by Pastor Hans Christian Lier who had taken in the refugee from the hospital and led him to Christ.

Still living on what he called his 'borrowed time', Bjørn and Ann returned to Norway after two years to take on fresh Christian challenges. Bjørn himself spent time in Bible college and translating Christian books into Norwegian, before returning to the sea working on two of Norway's state passenger ships and then on a cargo ship in Madagascar off the coast of Africa, finally returning to Norway to work in the Ships' Research Institute.

His third heart operation followed—changing the artificial valve for a more modern type and the insertion of a pacemaker which steadied his heartbeat but reminded him once more of the fragility of his extended life. He stretched that fragility to its utmost, however, travelling to Israel for two long winter holidays and to Indonesia to visit his friends and cross Java by local bus, living life to the full. He spoke to a hall packed with two hundred sailors, telling them of the difference Jesus Christ had made to his own life.

Work in the research institute allowed him to retire early, though retirement was not the appearance given as he merely flung himself into a fresh round of tasks such as revitalising the Emmaus Bible correspondence course in Norway, more Bible study (including learning Greek and Hebrew as an aid), taking a radio course so that he could do Christian radio work, helping with the Blue Cross work among alcoholics, and preaching in his local church regularly.

It was in the midst of this activity that it became apparent that Bjørn would need another operation. When a letter arrived from his doctor suggesting that a heart transplant was his only hope to improve his condition because of the rapidly deteriorating state of his own heart, he agreed to go for extensive tests to check if he was a suitable candidate.

'If the operation is successful it could give you back ninety-five per cent use of your strength,' he was told when accepted.

Bjørn was told to return home and wait until a suitable heart was available. A small personal-alarm was clipped to his pocket to warn him that he had twenty minutes before needing to leave for the hospital. A false alarm, when he and another patient reported together only for the other man to be given the heart, didn't deter Bjørn. He waited patiently. It was on 25 June 1987 that the call came—105 days after the search for a heart had begun. In the hospital Bjørn and Ann prayed together and then he was taken for surgery.

Shaved all over his body, X-rayed, examined carefully, and after his blood had been tested, he was wheeled under the arc lights of the operating theatre. Green-clad surgeons and assistants began the fight to extend his life. The scalpel sliced cleanly through the chest; hands and equipment began the operation that would replace his heart with a new one. Outside the theatre Ann waited, fearful and yet at the same time confident that her husband's life was in God's hands just as much as those of the medical team. From 6 p.m., when she had walked into the hospital alongside Bjørn, Ann waited, watching him being wheeled from the preparation ward into the operating theatre at ten minutes past eight.

At 3.30 the following morning her seven-hour wait was over; she watched Bjørn being taken into a sterile room where he was to be constantly moni-tored. Above the bed the green screen of the electro-cardiagram monitoring his heart blipped its encouraging jagged route; the drip feed bottles hung like sagging plastic sacks from their stands sending their contributions of help into his bloodstream, and all the while attendants gave her encouraging looks as they passed in and out of the room.

Bjørn recovered and Ann saw again the smile of confidence that had given her sixteen years of pleasure. They knew that from this operation there was no turning back: it would either be successful or it would not, and failure meant Bjørn's life was forfeit. They had considered the price worthwhile. 'Whatever happens God has given me my life back twice,' Bjørn told her. 'Once after my second heart operation and then he gave me spiritual life and that is what I value more than anything. I have no fears for the future—Jesus is with me wherever I am. Whether I live or die—I belong to the Lord.'

Dressed in green, loose-fitting hospital robes and with a mask covering his mouth and nose, George Verwer spent time with his friend six days after the operation, and as the visit of an elder from church two days later ended in prayer Bjørn turned and sang spontaneously in a strong voice, 'Turn your eyes upon Jesus, look full in his wonderful face, and the things of earth will grow strangely dim in the light of his glory and grace.'

On 11 July—sixteen days after the operation— Bjørn Kristiansen died. After six days of intensive medical and surgical activity the constantly flickering graph mark on the green screen of the heart monitor settled into a constant line. At the age of fifty-three Bjørn went to meet the Saviour who had changed his life twenty years previously.

On one of those nights while that final struggle with life was taking place Ann sat in the waiting room accompanied by a nurse. 'There is a nurse who is a Christian and belongs to the Salvation Army who told me about your husband,' the nurse told Ann. 'She said, "If ever you get an opportunity talk to Bjørn Kristiansen about his life and how he became a Christian." Last night I was on duty in his room and we talked for two hours about his faith in Jesus Christ and he told me how to become a Christian.'

The small church in Oslo was packed with people including that last enquiring nurse, the Salvation Army nurse, a transplant patient who had met Bjørn in the hospital, and other people Bjørn had shared his new life with. But it was no hour of gloom. The hymns, chosen by Bjørn while waiting for the call to hospital, were cheerful reminders of the power of the gospel. The white coffin wearing a white ribbon bearing the words 'Absent from the body—present with the Lord' was afterwards carried to the cemetery overlooking the green fields of Bjørn's beloved country, the sweeping meadows giving way to woodland. It contained nothing but the body which had taken Bjørn to hospital. The soul, the real man, was already in heaven beginning another new chapter . . .

3

Isabelle: A study in faith

The petite figure of Isabelle walked into the grey, forbidding block that was the Sorbonne, Paris's premier university, swinging her bag and enjoying life. She pushed aside the massive glass-panelled door and made straight for the largest of the three desks. Standing in front of the desk she waited for the clerk—also larger than anyone else in the room—to look up. When she had her attention the 20-year-old student spoke: 'I would like the forms for my first year of research, please.'

The clerk reached into a cabinet, slid open the drawer and handed across the form. 'You realise it has to be in by this afternoon if you want to sit that paper this year?' she pointed out.

Isabelle's face dropped. 'Pardon?'

The statement was repeated. 'It has to be back today.' The clerk could see the anxiety on the young girl's face and began to be helpful. 'What did you want to take? . . . There probably isn't a problem.'

Isabelle was perplexed. About to begin her research year, she knew that students were usually

given three or four weeks in which to select the
subject and professor under which they would take
their twelve months' study. Just a few days ago,
chatting to friends in a café, she had heard that it
had surprisingly been reduced to a fortnight—not a
lot of time in which to make the necessary arrangements—and now she was being told that she had
just a matter of hours to finalise the decision on
which her year's study and its important thesis
would hang. There was no alternative, however;
she knew she had to make an instant selection or
delay her studies a year—unthinkable! The rent for
her Paris flat and her living expenses depended on
getting through the year with distinction; that way
she could maintain the special student-teacher's
grant she had been given. She did no teaching, it
was one of the educational system's ways of giving
grants, providing Isabelle taught for ten years afterwards.

She thought hurriedly: she wanted to study Plato
with Mme Jacqueline de Romilly, a specialist in
Greek literature. Even as Isabelle voiced her desires
she sensed the answer that was going to come back
from the other side of the desk.

'I'm sorry, but Mme de Romilly is on holiday
and won't be back for a week or so. That means she
will be unable to sign your application.'

There was no time to feel numb with annoyance
as Isabelle could have done. The professor taking
the final year had to sign the papers, so she had to
find a professor who was available—and who
taught a subject in which she was interested.

Within minutes the helpful clerk had listed several professors, their subjects, and the rooms in

which they could be found. Isabelle rushed on her way, her placid entrance minutes before a thing of the past. She hurtled through the enormous, high-vaulted corridors, peeping into rooms and discovering areas of the Sorbonne she had never noticed in the two years she had been studying there. But even as she raced on her way, prospects began to slither from her grasp.

The first professor, with whom she considered taking modern French literature, was fully committed; he could take no more students—'I'm sorry.'

Round the enormous twisting flights of stairs she clambered, but each time finding a refusal: either the professor was booked up, or wasn't available.

Desperately she made her way back to the reception office. 'Who is left?' she pleaded.

The clerk checked her records. 'The only professor available that I know about is Madame Harl . . .' the words and room number were hardly out of her mouth before Isabelle's flight began again. She now had just one hour to complete her application. Over the bridge spanning two sections of the Sorbonne she raced, up stairs and down more passages until she gasped her way to the top of the building, a door in one of the tiny turrets poking its way above the roof-top.

Nervously she knocked on the door, realising as she did so that she had no idea what subjects Madame Harl covered and what would be expected of her. All she knew was the final warning words which had trailed after her as she left the main office . . . 'She should be able to take you . . . it's such a hard subject and not many people are interested . . .'

As the door opened she was faced by a short, well-dressed woman, with a pleasant smile and a friendly welcome. Isabelle introduced herself and tried to fish for the subject matter that might become important to her. 'I am doing my first research-year diploma and would like to do it with you. What would you advise?'

Madame Harl smiled. 'You're a brave student. Few come to me because it is so difficult.'

What could it be? pounded Isabelle's heart. As they talked it became evident that Madame Harl dealt with biblical subjects linked with post-classical Greek. Isabelle's heart sank: her Bible knowledge was restricted to stories of the saints she had read as a child, and all the Greek studies she had done had been in the classical period only. But she had no option. It had to be this.

'That sounds fascinating,' was all she could think of to say. Then Madame Harl began to complete her form and discussed the particular subject for the major thesis. She had, she explained, an old manuscript in Greek which Isabelle could translate and write a commentary on. She inscribed the title of the subject on Isabelle's form: 'The interpretation of the Fathers of the Church of Psalm 119 verse 62, and the "mesonuktion" (midnight office) among Greek monks in the fourth century.' Isabelle breathed her thanks and made her hasty way back to the office to hand in her form. As she did so the enormity of what she was doing hit her: she was launching into the examination of a book she knew nothing about in a language she might hardly understand. But there was no doubt in her mind, she had no alternative. It was what she had worked for all her twenty years, and the Master's Degree was what she so badly needed.

Short, dark-haired and attractive, Isabelle had been destined for a higher education almost from birth. Her French father had had to give up a coffee plantation he owned in Saigon, just a couple of years after his daughter was born, because of the war, and Isabelle was taken to France to live with her grandmother. Life in the countryside outside Marseille was pleasant, and Isabelle soon proved herself to be a clever pupil and exceptionally keen to learn.

At four years old she could read, write and preferred books to her dolls. She learnt her reading on Grandmother's knee alongside the fireplace in their home, watching the characters with her eyes as Grandmother moved a steady finger along while she read aloud. When Isabelle began to read the words herself Grandmother just laughed and assumed she was memorising them from the pictures. But as soon as the youngster started school she realised it wasn't the case: she was genuinely clever.

The teachers found her a willing pupil, invariably top of the class, and the winner of many of the prizes for achievement in the form, the school or even the district educational authority.

At the local grammar school they even invented special IQ tests to stretch her mind and keep her occupied. By the time she was seven Isabelle was reading the stories of the Saints, handed to her by her Roman Catholic grandmother, Marie Javoukey; the patron saint of Paris, Saint Geneviève, and Thérèsa de Lisieux being her favourites.

She also loved the life story of Albert Schweitzer because he was musical, loved life, travelled a lot, and used his knowledge to help others.

When she was eight she moved to live with an aunt in a different area of Marseille. Her aunt, a teacher herself, lived in a large house provided by the school which meant that Isabelle had her own bedroom—and her own study with its desk and book-lined walls. Even so she still frequented her aunt's library, raiding classics and other literature to devour in her free time.

Something inside Isabelle drove her to learn. It certainly wasn't the aunt, who tried to ensure that the constant praise from school didn't go to her niece's head. The aunt didn't drive, so much as allow Isabelle the latitude to study and provide the environment in which learning was a pleasure.

At seventeen Isabelle went to university in Aix en Provence north of Marseille, the district's premier university. For a year she studied there taking classics, Latin, Greek and French in her stride. She had been directed towards Latin and Greek in her previous schools simply to give her something extra to concentrate on. Dull and uninterested, she absorbed them without a lot of feeling. 'What's the point?' she often said to her friends. 'Latin and Greek are dead languages—they are hardly used now. What good will they be to me?'

But she accepted her aunt's advice that, unlikely as it seemed, they would be helpful in gaining her qualifications as a teacher, and teaching was a useful, worthwhile, and secure profession. To please her aunt Isabelle didn't argue but simply studied on. It was, after all, good character-building material—however irrelevant.

She proved herself an able student, taking her A-levels two years early at sixteen, with a philosophy course thrown in, again to give her mind something extra to consider.

Eventually she was offered a prized place at the Sorbonne—more than six hundred years old and disputing with Bologna the claim to be the oldest university in Europe. Synonymous with the faculty of theology—it began life as a college for poor theological students when it was started by Robert de Sorbon, the chaplain to Louis IX—it had developed over the years, becoming the official headquarters of the University of Paris in 1821, but it was to gain a reputation of a different kind during the student rebellion of 1968, the year before Isabelle's studies finished.

It was to be an exciting new stage in the life of the girl determined to be a top student. She decided to specialise in the classical side of literature—French, Latin and Greek, and became immediately immersed in a sea of books, many from the pre-twentieth century, as she began to conquer the linguistic problems of the older-style languages.

But there were other diversions when Isabelle moved to Paris. Her aunt had rented a small flat for her in the Latin quarter of the city, a short walk from the sombre shadow of the Sorbonne itself, and she began to enjoy the theatres with their new plays, trips with new friends, and a social life which suddenly expanded on all fronts. Even then the serious student would find it difficult to fully comprehend why all her friends and those people she knew of her own age seemed to take life so light-heartedly.

There was one other reason why she felt compelled to stick at her work and do it so well: she had been given a student-teacher grant which was used to refund a loan she had obtained for her flat and gave her a regular, if small, allowance. But it depended on her getting a distinction during each of the four years she was a student at the Sorbonne. It was, she admitted, a real incentive not to make too many mistakes.

Isabelle began to be fascinated by the classical material she was studying. Plato was particularly puzzling: he maintained, she read, that man was a creature driven by two horses—one a white beast pulling upwards and the other a black animal pulling downwards. There was always the fight between good and evil. She tried to decide in her mind whether he was right. He also pictured life as being like a man in a cave, looking at images projected on the bottom of a pit, while light and reality are behind him and far above him. But to succeed the man had to turn his back on what was happening in the picture and climb up the back of the cave wall, until he discovered a way to the sunlight and true life. It was all so mysterious.

St Augustine was just as much of a frustration. He had a favourite phrase, 'love, and then do what you want.' It sounded very much as though he were advocating a completely free life, but Isabelle knew it wouldn't be that. He was too genuinely good to mean that. It must be so profound that she could not understand it. He must, she considered, have found a dimension in life that was completely outside her sphere of experience.

The oriental religions and occult also intrigued her, introducing her to a spiritual world which she found puzzling in an intellectually curious way. When she dabbled in astrology she was told by one leading exponent that she was extremely gifted and talented in that direction. 'I can teach you to make a profession of it,' he promised. 'Put off your studies and come and learn from me.' She considered the invitation but decided to put it off until another time . . . but such a time never came.

But life in Paris and at the Sorbonne was all she hoped it would be: exciting, challenging, mind-stretching and with plenty of life in the city to appeal to her youthful love of classical entertainment.

The Latin quarter, the south bank of the Seine, was a wonderland of fascination; small streets, majestic buildings, lively discussions in smoky bistros and a youthful vigour which presented her with a whole spectrum of life she had not come into contact with before. Then there was the variety of museums and libraries; a lure for someone with Isabelle's love for reading.

Now that same enthusiasm for learning had brought her to the greatest challenge of her young life: her year of research at the Sorbonne. When the panic of her last-minute application had subsided, and she had time to consider what she had let herself in for, Isabelle was worried, but confident. She had, after all, always been near the top.

Then Madame Harl presented her with the ultimate challenge. A sheet of photocopy paper contained a small facsimile of the one verse from the Bible that was to take every scrap of intellectual inquisitiveness Isabelle could muster. The A4 sheet had just a little group of Greek letters clustered in the centre—about six centimetres wide by three centimetres deep. Scrawled by monks in the fourth century, it had so far been ignored by scholars who had other manuscripts to work on. Discovered in the Dead Sea region of Israel—not far from Qumran where the Dead Sea Scrolls were first found by a young shepherd hunting for his goats— the remnant was small, but contained a massive challenge. Madame Harl, a lay specialist in the Bible, had been presented with it to research and now part of that was to be done by Isabelle.

For three months, however, she got more and more frustrated as the mysteries of the document eluded her. Often she almost reached breaking-point, nearly giving up her studies, so perplexed was she by the writing, some of it obviously missing and other small sections crossed out and rewritten. The language—Greek—was very different from the classical style she had previously studied. And the scrap on which it had been written was now torn, adding to the confusion.

As Isabelle gazed at the fragment and tried to fathom out its meaning, the weight of its importance couldn't fail to hit her: her whole future was balanced on a small scrap of parchment and a few words scrawled in Greek by a monk something like sixteen hundred years ago in Israel. Only the knowledge that to give up would lose her her grant, her flat and her future kept her working.

Desperate for help, she confronted Madame Harl after three months. 'I'm getting nowhere,' she said. But the kindly answer pointed her in the direction of reinforcements. She met Cardinal Daniélou, a specialist in the Bible, and other students chipped in with helpful information. She began to look at the Septuagint—the ancient Greek translation of the Old Testament—and the Greek Fathers of the Church and their writings, to try and understand their minds and circumstances.

Jerome, the translator of the Vulgate—the Bible in Latin—who lived in a cave underneath the Church of the Nativity in Bethlehem, was one to whose writings she turned for inspiration. And the writings of the monks began to expose Isabelle to their peculiar life-style, which seemed strange and yet became magnetic, as it opened up to her the world of the times when the verse she was looking at was written.

The verse itself, she discovered, was Psalm 119 verse 62: 'In the middle of the night I wake up to praise you for your righteous judgments.' One sentence—but one which kept her awake at night also, as she fathomed out the depth of its meaning.

It occurred in the longest of all the 150 psalms—an unusual psalm, with every one of its 176 verses mentioning in one way or another the Word of God, or the Bible, or God's commandments.

Her task, to translate the verse and write a commentary on it, was an enormous one. The commentary took months, and then she began to understand its meaning. The key, she felt, was in the lives of the monks—they were so holy and wanted so much to please God that they took the verse literally and would get up in the middle of the night for a service. Night-time, she knew herself, was a time of temptation, of fear, of punishment or persecution; whether for one soul, a group of believers or a whole nation. So the monks had to turn to God—a God of love and mercy—and listen to him.

She began to read the Bible, studying the Hebrew and Greek and examining the ancient texts to picture the world in which the ancient monks lived, and sense the air they breathed. To them, she knew, Christianity was the meaning of life—part of the warfare against demons which they knew existed.

For Isabelle it was as if she had turned her educational clock back: she felt like a child put in a class above its level of intelligence, struggling for meaning and thought patterns. But gradually, bit by bit, it began to drop into place.

She became friendly with the proprietors of a local Bible shop in the Latin Quarter, buying her English, Greek and Hebrew Bibles there and chatting to the staff who were interested in her project—and also, she discovered, interested in her as a person. The sense of awe which they had for the Bible had begun to rub off on Isabelle, not simply from their conversations but primarily from her reading of the book itself.

It could not have a normal author behind it, she reasoned; it was something greater than just good literature. As an avid reader and student of the classics she sensed something different and extra in the book; that something extra put a dimension into her studies she had not expected to gain when she began.

Isabelle had made her way over Pont Neuf across the Seine and round the massive walls of the Louvre to the Palais Royal. Skirting the walls of the Palais between the Banque de France, she walked to the national library—the Bibliotheque Nationale. Ranking with London's British Library as one of the two largest in Western Europe, the rambling buildings had already proved a treasure-trove to the earnest student. Through the glass doors she entered the reading-room—seating three hundred and sixty readers with access to more than ten thousand volumes—and booked her seat.

The quiet scholarly atmosphere was something she loved and she perched at the small desk, her privacy guaranteed to a limited extent by the carved wooded sides of the desk, which rose on either side of her. A table lamp cast its glow over the papers and books she soon spread over the surface of the desk, and she began to study the Bible as she had on a number of occasions before.

This time, however, the grandeur of the book, and its majestic power, suddenly struck her. She saw not just a book, or even a collection of stories, but a volume inspired in some miraculous way by God. Some amazing power had given life to the people whose stories she was reading. She was, by now, familiar with the call of Abraham and the way he settled in Canaan with his nomadic family—the birth of God's chosen people. She had read of how, through famine, they had been led into Egypt and then miraculously taken out by Moses under the inspiration of God's guidance. 'This book doesn't have the spirit of a normal author,' she said to herself. 'This is something greater—God, the Holy Spirit, really has inspired it. God, who created all things, had a personal hand in the lives and experiences of ordinary people because he loved them.

'This,' she mused, 'is something far greater than I know.'

Suddenly an outside power began to fill her. She began shaking, inwardly, unaware of anyone in the reading-room. The power of God, the power that she had been reading about, gripped her and began to shake her. It was a crushing power—yet one that would not crush her, she knew. She felt God was close, talking to her, filling her with his love. She felt awestruck—respectful, and yet at the same time realising that despite his creative ability and eternal vantage point, God was making it very plain that he loved her, a French student, and wanted to be her personal friend.

The God, whom she had imagined always addressed her as Miss Dumeyni, began to call her Isabelle. He was that close. The circle of light from the reading-room and the papers on her desk, even the lofty setting of the room, were lost as she felt herself lifted into the presence of Almighty God.

It was an experience Isabelle didn't forget. Her studies continued—she gained her Master's Degree and became a teacher—but parallel with that intellectual research came a realisation that God was real. For some years it was, she discovered later, an intellectual awareness and a mental assent. But as she increased her friendship with the folk in the Christian bookstall, and began to attend more of their meetings in a small hall alongside the shop, or on Sundays in a larger, rented room at the nearby engineering school, niggling little incidents began to expose the paucity of her faith.

A lady she met who attended the Salvation Army meetings radiated the sort of peace Isabelle longed for, but somehow couldn't capture in all her research or church attendance. Just being near the

woman was a joy—on one occasion Isabelle wrote a
song after one such meeting, she was so inspired.
And deep down she began to realise something was
missing in her life: she had accepted that there was
a God and that he loved her, but now she had
noticed that the elderly lady brought with her a
freshness and radiance that was different to anything Isabelle had experienced.

Even baptism in the church, where they assumed
she was a devout Christian because she said the
right words and did the right actions, failed to
satisfy the growing awareness inside Isabelle's
heart that all was not right.

She knew now that she could not earn her own
forgiveness and acceptance with God—that had
been done by Jesus, God's Son, when he died for
her on the Cross. But for Isabelle, used to earning
everything in life by her own hard work, this was
particularly difficult to accept. And so that final
step of faith—simply to believe in what God had
done for her—remained beyond her.

It was to be ten years after her experience in the
library that she finally gave in. During those years
she became a teacher, married and had two sons.
During a time of marital crisis she was in her bedroom on a day off from work in school, when she
had a second deep experience with God. Looking
out of the window she saw the trees and grass of a
beautiful spring day. The freshness of it all made
her fall to her knees in tears, suddenly seeing herself
as God saw her—a woman who had tried hard to
be a Christian in her own strength and had followed
her own passions. As the tears flowed, an unusual
experience for Isabelle, she felt the love of Jesus

Christ filling her. His compassion encompassed her life and she knew that her pleas for forgiveness had been heard. In an instant, it seemed, life began anew with all the enthusiasm of the flowers she could see forcing their way through to demonstrate the coming of spring.

For Isabelle, Jesus had brought spring. Now she knew she was a Christian. 'It was,' she explained to a close friend, 'rather like a scientific experiment and just as conclusive. Experiments with the same elements always give similar results—so it is with God. He loves us all and I suddenly realised, years after first accepting that he was real, that he loved me really, warmly, dazzlingly and cared so much for me. Now life is very different.'

The student had learnt life's biggest and most valuable lesson, and it all started when she was given a miniature scrap of manuscript written sixteen hundred years ago by a monk in a far-off land.

4

Pavel: A lieutenant surrenders

Huddling on the carpet with the arms of his father round him, Pavel watched through the window the flashes of rockets exploding in the street. His younger brother was alongside him and his mother lay nearby. Father had positioned them alongside the thickest wall in the Czechoslovakian house after seeing Russian tanks and armoured cars arriving in the town.

To Pavel, aged nine, and his brother, it was exciting. The darkness of the room was illuminated by the occasional light of a rocket and the explosion made his mother shake and bury her head deep in her arms. Father had earlier peered through the doorway but quickly retreated to the safety of the inner room with the message that a Russian half-track vehicle was stationed in the town square at the end of the road. A grey-clad soldier was sitting on the top cuddling a machine gun to his chin, aiming up and down the street and occasionally pulling back the trigger to allow a stream of bullets to sing viciously against walls and through windows.

From his bedroom window earlier in the day—21 August 1968—Pavel had seen the Russians arrive in Slovakia in their high-speed push from Poland, and watched in horror as an old lady had been shot as she scurried quickly from one wall to the next, trying to avoid their cruel and deadly games. She was to die unaided in the road that had been as familiar to her as her home.

The night was spent on the floor. Father hurried upstairs and brought down a supply of blankets and a mattress on which they crowded, using the wall as their protective shield while the noise of gunfire eased. Pavel fell asleep—a small boy for whom excitement came in ways that adults could not accept.

As daylight poured through the same window that only hours before had shown military might, Pavel got ready for school. His parents insisted he went, much to his chagrin and despite the roaming groups of soldiers, the red epaulettes on their dingy grey suits a reminder of the blood he had seen spilt.

Outside he raced to the town square to squabble with friends over the brass shells still lying where they had been spewed from the machine gun. Later he was to learn that a 5-year-old boy had died— a victim of the explosive power of one of those shells—when the bullet had ricocheted into his room and struck him in bed. The houses were pockmarked with lines of holes, torn from the plaster and brickwork by the soldier's late-night game. Fragments of pottery lay on the pavements with an occasional flower peering woefully from scattered earth—a reminder that the soldier had been testing his aim against the window boxes and pot plants decorating the windows.

At school the teacher—a young woman—was stern. 'If they had come with open hands we would have welcomed them,' she said. 'But they came with guns . . . only bringing trouble.' Weeks later as the occupation continued the young boy noticed that her story changed; the Russians were welcomed as saviours, anxious to bring better and more prosperous days to his native land. The First Secretary of the Communist Party, Alexander Dubcek, had been spirited to Moscow to pay the price of the Prague Spring, a balmy six months during which he had tried to shrug off his country's dependence on the Soviet Union to a more controlled neutrality.

Czechoslovakia in 1968 was not a good place to be. But for Pavel it was home. It was all he had. As a promising child he was to shine in school lessons and was eventually invited to apply for a place in one of the Military High Schools—it was an honour even to be identified as a possible candidate. His parents were excited: though it meant Pavel leaving home, it was the best possible education and meant he had a permanent future.

So one summer's day the 15-year-old was placed on a train for the 350-kilometre ride to his new life. Apprehensive and full of foreboding, and yet with a tinge of excitement, Pavel settled into the carriage, his meagre possessions in a bag on the luggage rack. His eyes scanned the train for other raw recruits. He sensed that one or two of the teenagers might be heading for the same place, but his shyness prevented him asking. Some, he noticed, soon got into conversation with each other; he remained in the corner of his compartment watching the Czech countryside slide by.

He had tried a lot of things already in his young life to find fulfilment; perhaps the new school and army life would bring it.

He thought of the time he had taken up judo with Jan, a friend in the ninth grade at school. Jan said he was a Christian and did judo and karate. He also dabbled in yoga which he claimed brought him nearer to God. Pavel tried. It was true, he discovered. He began to learn how to relax and meditate. He was told to think of infinity—to allow his mind to empty—then he had to try and imagine his mind leaving his body. His yoga was linked with the judo classes and he also had to visualise a fight before it happened—'Try to run through the fight in your mind and anticipate all your opponent's moves, allowing your body to move even before the mind tells it,' said the instructor. It was difficult. But Pavel persisted—he wanted to be the best; that was part of his life.

It was his introduction to eastern mysticism and religions. As he advanced in the thought-forms, he was instructed in how to allow the snake power to take over his mind. Snake power, he was told, was the highest form, and he began to surrender to its influence. However, as it tightened its hold in him, with all the strength of a boa constricting its prey, Pavel realised he would have to give it up. It was taking over his body, even overpowering his speech organs. His sessions with the snake power ended with him feeling drained, feeling as if his throat was under the control of an outside influence.

He lay gasping on his bed for hours unable to help himself. 'It's wrong, I know it is,' he told himself. 'My dreams are evil and I must escape this power.'

He gave up the classes and gradually the evil influence left him. But he still toyed with yoga . . .

Now, sitting in the train bound for the military school, he allowed his mind to drain and tried to free himself of the worries and concerns which racked his excited young brain.

The train stopped with a jolt; it was time to leave. As he struggled from the platform he realised that the fifteen or so youngsters around him were all making their way to the same place. It was some sort of comfort. The high wire fence straggled round the school complex, and the enormous gates, guarded by young soldiers only a year or so older than himself, seemed menacing rather than welcoming.

Inside the huge entrance hall the fifteen boys appeared lost, miniature figures against the towering pillars and imposing architecture. On each side passages ran away, threatening and gloomy. The boys were taken into a dining room where they tucked into food, not wanting to eat because of the gnawing excitement, yet still recognising they had teenage appetites to satisfy. Once they had begun to thaw and chat around the highly polished tables, an officer appeared to order them to their rooms.

As names were called they followed the pointing truncheon of the officer. Pavel meekly walked in the direction indicated to find a dormitory lined with two-tier bunk beds, each containing a handwritten

name-plate. His was a top bunk and alongside the
name was a neat pile of clothing: a deep-blue track
suit, forage-cap, underclothes, and a pair of green
training shoes that was to be his working uniform
for the next four years.

Later he would be measured for, and receive, the
smart green uniform with a peaked cap, for use on
more formal occasions. The cap had a badge on the
front—the national symbol—on a gold background. It looked smart and made him feel proud.

Fingering the blue track suit he heard the same
officer who had guided them towards the dormitory
issuing the next orders. They were to report to the
medical room for examination. Naked boys stood
under the scrutiny of medical officers . . . and then,
clothed again, reported to the barber to have their
hair cut short. Pavel watched in the mirror as his
hair began to fall around his neck until only a short,
prickly crew cut remained. It was somehow soul-
destroying; he felt that part of him was being
attacked.

In the days that followed he discovered the truth
in that initial observation. Made to move quickly
from their six o'clock awakening, ablutions, breakfast and tidying the dormitory, to the lectures,
everything was done on the double. The boys were
made to run from one task to another; it was a
gradual effort to rob them of individuality and
create a puppet-like reliance on the military system.

The education included much of what took place
in the normal Czech schools but here there was
always the extra stress on political awareness and
ideology. Pavel began to realise that not only were
the constant orders designed to create instant

obedience but the teaching was directing all the youngsters towards the same goal: to become Communist 'clones'.

'It is a sophisticated system, but I feel myself being gradually changed. Only the fact that my spirit is strong prevents me being sucked into the system like the other boys I have observed,' he told his parents on a rare visit home. 'I am being robbed of the freedom to think for myself.'

Pavel, like the others, wasn't allowed to go anywhere without permission—not even the toilet. It was degrading and soul-destroying. He would often sit on his bed and stare at the row of grey metal wardrobes lining the walls of the dormitory and dream of life in his little town. But it was a dream that could not be fulfilled, as the youngster gradually realised.

He listened as the lecturers tried to twist history into their own political ideals. One army corporal was the history teacher. His lessons about the country's founder and first president, Thomas Mazaryk, were at variance from what Pavel had been told by his father and others. He had looked upon the president, who had proclaimed the new republic in Prague in 1918, as a friend of Czechoslovakia; loved by and devoted to his people. But now he learnt that the president had been trying to create a 'little America' in which only a few people would be well off and the remainder would suffer. Holiday talks with his father convinced Pavel it was a prejudiced view. True, Mazaryk had had an American wife but he had spent four years, and on two occasions almost given up, trying to build the republic to help the people of his homeland.

It seemed, thought Pavel, the lecturer had forgotten that Karl Marx had once said, 'An historical misfortune places the Czechs on the side of the Russians, on the side of despotism against revolution.'

Other lessons carried the same bias. Despite the fact that Pavel had always ignored the huge family Bible which lay on the table in his home, he couldn't accept it when one major, smartly dressed in his green uniform and wearing the gold epaulettes and star of office, pointed out that although a few people still believed in God in Czechoslovakia, they were few and far between and Christianity was all over. There was no future in it. The Communist system had proved itself more capable of satisfying the needs of mankind. Lectures on Marx and Lenin followed, ideologies which had never struck Pavel as any more satisfactory than the Christianity of which he knew little and proposed to learn nothing.

But he enjoyed the more practical soldier-oriented courses. Friday mornings always brought a practical soldiering course which he relished. One week the lads sat through a lecture on how First World War trenches were cut; then they were issued with sharp, pointed army spades and told to go out and dig some. They scooped out fox-holes, flinging themselves into them to escape from mock explosions and then dug a long trench, racing back and forth pretending to be hiding from an enemy; although any adversary would have had few problems scaling the shallow results of their work.

The boys were also given hand-grenades and shown how to withdraw the firing pins and throw

them. Pavel cautiously pulled the pin, arched his
back, straightened his hand and flung the grenade
away to watch it explode harmlessly in the distance.
He was exhilarated. They were not real but the
explosions certainly seemed authentic.

That was even more true when they were made
to practise in a dummy minefield. The students
were sent in small teams to walk through the
minefield, carefully picking their way between what
they thought were mines. Occasionally a fearful
explosion and the sudden squeal of a startled teen-
ager indicated that a mistake had been made.
Although they weren't real explosives it was scary
enough for Pavel.

After they had gingerly managed to cross the
field they were given lessons in how to dismantle
the mines. If they didn't slip the fuse out neatly the
mine's detonation would give them a headache but
no worse damage. 'At least none blew up on me,'
Pavel wrote home. But he didn't tell his parents
how he had almost jumped from his track suit when
the bomb being examined alongside him had suddenly crashed into life.

That apart, Pavel did not like school. The first
year simply confirmed his distaste; the second year
began to turn into hatred of the system. By the third
year he was using his summer holiday to plead with
his parents to get him out. They tried, but the
results of their enquiries shocked them. The
application form signed by their 15-year-old son
had put him in the army for life: the military college
was merely the first stage. They could buy him out
but it would cost something like fifteen thousand
crowns for each year—plus paying for clothing,

education and food. The price was too high. Pavel's
mother tried other short-cuts but each one ended in
failure. He was in the army and he would have to
stay.

There was also the knowledge that if he did leave,
he would be blacklisted from joining any other
school, and his education would come to a stand-
still. Life suddenly took on a very grim appearance
for the 17-year-old soldier-boy.

During Pavel's final year there was even more
disappointment. When he had joined the academy
he was promised that afterwards there would be the
opportunity of getting an entrance into the medical
side of army life or even flying school. Instead he
was given no option: this school was directing its
pupils towards tank regiments to boost the country's intake. The only alternative was the rocket
side. A keen electronics student, Pavel opted for
that.

Life was presenting him with one disaster after
another. A good student, he was to have little say in
his future. Once in the army he realised he had sold
his body and future to the authorities.

As college life ended Pavel faced another stage of
his career: he was sent to a radio station which
specialised in tracking satellites and also kept a
watching brief on Western missile bases in West
Germany and Austria. Now a lieutenant, he was in
charge of a unit of forty of the workers on the base
with ultimate power over them. And he knew how
vital the work was to the security of his nation and
the USSR, for whom the observations were being
kept. The station was one in a chain of such out-
posts along the Czech border, keeping the West
under permanent observation.

Radio messages were constantly being received and sent by satellite, needles monotonously stroking the radar screens, giving a continuous picture of the areas under observation. He studied continuously, needing to be aware of the trajectory of any missile and what that could mean in terms of range and distance. The work was interesting and varied, and being in charge of a section gave Pavel the authority to at least carve out a niche for himself. He was good at the job. The only thing he jibbed at—and then never in public—was the constant political lectures he had to give his men. 'I have this thick book that I have to work through, lecturing the men from, but it is full of lies. I don't believe it,' he told his father. But he had to swallow his feelings and continue. It was, after all, his life.

The early awareness of eastern religions had led him to study Rama Krishna and that became another interest. The rules were simple: love life—but his army training and even the work he was engaged in made it difficult to live a life that was totally divorced from violent action or thought. It was better than some of the studies he had made into religion, but Pavel realised it was still not the answer.

His own father had been a Christian once but had given up his faith at the age of thirty—round about the time Pavel had been born. So although his father still enjoyed talking about God, the conversation never seemed very real to Pavel. After all, he thought, what's the point in believing something that doesn't affect you?

And Christianity, he reasoned, ought to affect a person. While Pavel wouldn't go all the way with the major who debunked it as an 'old woman's religion—certainly not for anyone in his right mind,' he was still tempted to think that the major's remarks contained a bit of truth.

A magazine article laid the groundwork for Pavel's next religious experience—the story of Ghandi. The Indian statesman had had a fascinating life and Pavel got other books, gradually studying the life of this pacifist leader of a nation. It seemed new and real. It appeared to work. He read of how Ghandi and hundreds of others had lain down in front of a British train to make one point and it had worked. Constantly Ghandi's actions had been full of gentleness and love. He noticed that Ghandi loved reading the Sermon on the Mount from the Bible. That sparked off a fresh interest, and Pavel decided he ought to find out something about Christianity—but real Christianity, not the out-dated version that attracted only old women to church. He needed to find a vibrant, living Christian and talk it through.

But who was there in an atheistic, Communist country who could tell him about God? He talked to friends, delicately phrasing his questions until he realised he was speaking to someone who went to church occasionally. The man's life didn't fit but he did know a Christian. 'It's Millan—you know, the young man in your own section,' he was told. 'He goes to church regularly—and reads a Bible.'

Pavel enquired and discovered the young man was in the shower room. Within minutes he had crashed the door open and strode in. Millan looked round to see why the door had been thrust open with such abruptness and, seeing it was his boss, he

attempted a half-hearted salute one-handed, allowing the towel to fall from his waist as he did so. He
was left standing naked, grasping with one hand at
the towel which was drifting down his side. Pavel
called out: 'You are a Christian. I want to talk to
you about it—now!' Millan began to shake, and not
just from the chilly air which had been let into the
room.

'Can I get dressed first, Sir?' he asked. Pavel
stood impatiently tapping his foot as the young man
dressed and then, as Millan tried to wipe the con-
densation from the lenses of his spectacles, briskly
led the way out of the shower room for their conversation.

Pavel made for the only room he knew they could
use without interruption: the small operations
room, used only once a month for practice drill.
After getting the key he let himself in and allowed
Millan to enter before clicking the lock. Radio
receivers lined one wall, silent; another wall was
covered with radar screens, the dullness of their
lifeless images in contrast to the turmoil in Pavel's
mind. Millan was obviously frightened: he had no
idea why his boss had suddenly decided to quiz him
about his faith, and it scared him.

'I want to know about Christianity. I have been
searching all my life for truth, for the meaning of life
and now I want to know about God,' Pavel burst
out. He gave Millan no chance to answer as he
continued: 'I have tried yoga, meditation, Rama
Krishna, and other things—please tell me about
God. I have tried to find him but without success. I
need something to satisfy me deep inside and
nothing I have tried so far has succeeded in doing

so. I know about the New Testament and I know about miracles—and I believe them. I know most people don't think things like that can happen but I know they can: after all, if evil things can happen like those that happened to me when I dabbled with the snake power, then I am certain there must be a good power in the world as well.'

Millan began to talk, gaining confidence as his fear left him and he realised that Pavel was in earnest; it wasn't a trick by his superior to trap him into revealing things about himself. He spoke of the state of the world, creation, and how, when God made it, man fell and began to sin. Then he talked of how God had already decided there was only one remedy for sin—the sacrifice of his own Son, Jesus Christ. 'And Jesus offered himself, came down to the earth to be born as a man and then, despite the good life he lived and the way he healed and helped people, he was crucified. He could have avoided it but refused to. Jesus knew it was the only way that you and I could have freedom to love God and worship him as his own sons.'

Pavel listened captivated. As Millan went on to explain how Jesus Christ had come into his own life and made a radical difference, changing it and giving him a new chance in life, Pavel knew he would have to learn more.

The next day Millan shyly approached his group leader with a small package. 'This might help you, Sir,' he said, hoping that the events of the previous day were not now forgotten. 'If you have any more questions please call me, Sir, I'll be glad to answer them.'

In the quietness of his office Pavel opened the package to discover a New Testament. From its well-used state it had obviously belonged to Millan himself. Pavel opened it immediately at the beginning and began to read Matthew's Gospel—it was fascinating. As the words sank into his heart he knew he was near the truth. The book was devoured like food; he read it at every opportunity and every difficult passage was referred to Millan. 'I began to think of myself as the most stupid person in the world with the number of questions I was asking,' he recalled later. 'But Millan was so calm and patient—I am sure anyone else would have given up on me. He didn't, it was another thing that convinced me that Christianity was true. No one could be like Millan unless he had exceptional power to draw on.'

Pavel also observed Millan's reactions in other areas: he didn't complain or get angry like his colleagues. As faith gently dawned in Pavel's heart he decided he ought to go to church. 'I must meet other Christians,' he told Millan. As a superior officer he arranged for Millan to have the following Sunday off, and agreed to go to church with the young man. Pavel dressed in civilian clothes and drove his own green Skoda to the church, parking a few streets away in case he was observed. As the pair walked into the dull, yellow-painted house which doubled as a church, he was impressed by the warm enthusiasm of everyone there. His hand was shaken so many times, and people looked genuinely pleased to see him. He was surprised by the welcome, but immediately he knew the atmosphere was different from anything else he had ever felt. He was given a song book and listened as the sixty or seventy people packed into the ground floor room sang. 'It was so beautiful,' he said afterwards.

The windows in the small building were open to allow the air to flow; it was a hot summer day. The congregation sat on wooden chairs, each with a hand-sewn cushion.

The pastor entered through a side door, an elderly, portly man, but with a radiant smile. 'He preached so simply—everything was so practical and easy to understand: he talked about the real world and real life and yet the life of Christ was in it. I was just touched by the message and felt peace in my heart and a great joy,' Pavel told Millan afterwards.

Pavel knew his search had ended. God was real to him. He gave up his eastern cults and began to immerse himself in the Bible, and loving God. 'In yoga everything goes out of a man—in Christianity God puts everything into a man,' he said. 'I just realised that God loved me and I wanted all of his love. I knew it was real.'

Some two years earlier Pavel had met and married a tall, attractive, brown-haired girl, Yula. She couldn't understand what had happened to him. 'What's happened?' she asked after that first day in church. Pavel tried to explain but she grinned and laughed it off. He had had so many fads; it was probably just another. But as the days and months went by she watched her husband and realised that it wasn't a passing fancy: it was real and he was a very different man. She began to go to church with Pavel and eventually decided to become a Christian herself. The couple had had a hard time together: they had met during an army exercise and for the first six months of their married life they had lived 420 kilometres apart. Eventually they had managed to get an army flat together and now lived in a state-owned flat near the radio centre.

Yula and Pavel began to pray about their future. Pavel knew the army was not the life he wanted but he could not think of a way out. He might have found a new life in Christ but there seemed no escape from the old life. As the couple prayed a verse of the Bible came to them both simultaneously—'Peace is what I leave with you; it is my own peace that I give you' (John 14:27).

'God is going to get you out of the army, Pavel, I know it,' said Yula. And Pavel felt the same confident stirring in his own heart.

He recalled a story his father had told him of how, when there was a danger of being drafted to the Russian front during the war, he was exempt because he had had a mystery illness for three months. When Pavel questioned officials he realised that this was one of the only ways out of the army— to have an illness that doctors couldn't cure or understand for three months. He made up his mind to fast. For weeks he refused to eat food, getting thinner and beginning to look weaker.

Just as he thought he might be able to use it to get out he was called before an army board. Marching in, Pavel assumed it was to answer questions on some of the radio work in which he had been engaged. He faced a row of medalled majors and waited for the first question.

'We understand you are going to church and are a Christian. Explain yourself,' he heard. The statement shook him. Now he was in real trouble. For someone in his position to own up to being a Christian could mean the end—disgrace—no future prospects. He felt far sicker than the effects of the fasting had managed to create. Suddenly he considered he was finished. His life had been discovered. They knew his secret. It wasn't worth defending himself. That decision made Pavel simply and truthfully explain his search for a meaning in life and how he had found true meaning in Jesus Christ.

'I didn't want to let God down,' he admitted afterwards to his wife. 'I told them everything. I just gave my testimony.' When he had finished he was ushered from the room while the verdict was reached.

Called back, Pavel faced the sombre trio. 'We've heard your story,' the major in the centre went on. 'You are a hard worker, and very good at your job. We don't want to lose you. We intend to help you a little to be a better soldier.'

Pavel was aghast. They were going to take away from him some of the jobs he didn't enjoy doing— but he would stay in the army.

It wasn't the solution he wanted, but what could he do? As he and Yula prayed about the situation they realised they could do nothing other than leave it in God's hands. 'It is his problem—I am his child,' Pavel decided.

Within weeks a letter arrived at his home. It looked official and with trembling hands he tore it open, and read with growing amazement. His face broke into an enormous grin as he rushed to find his wife. 'Read this, read this!' he shouted. Yula's face too betrayed her excitement as she read the terse document. The letter, received on a Thursday, told Pavel that on the following Tuesday he would no longer be in the army. God had performed another miracle.

The couple lost their flat but were given accommodation with the local pastor who had been Pavel's constant help. Yula, told by a doctor previously that she could not have children, suddenly became pregnant and the couple now have a lovely 20-month-old son.

Pavel, now a good-looking 30-year-old man working in electronics, reflects on his life. 'Life is not easy—but we have Jesus Christ. Our country might not allow us to worship with the freedom others do but we still love God and are thrilled to worship him. He has given me a new life, a wife, a baby, and a whole new future. What more could a man expect? I am free inside and God has taken me out of one army and made me a soldier in his.'

5

Stefan: Diagnosis—AIDS

AIDS! The four letters sent a shiver of fear through Stefan's frame as he stared across the desk at the notes the doctor was cautiously slipping back into their folder. The remainder of the medical report had been written with the sort of skill which doctors perfect—unreadable to anyone else, even the correct way up. But there had been no mistaking that final word, written in capitals and underlined. Stefan knew it could spell death. His!

The neat, clinical office in a hospital in eastern Switzerland was forgotten as his confused, shocked mind tried to pretend he hadn't seen it. A white overall held tight over his portly stomach, the doctor clipped the file together. 'We'll see what we can do,' he said reassuringly. 'The best thing would be to keep you here.' No mention was made of the word AIDS.

Mechanically the 22-year-old was led back to a waiting car and driven away. The town of Herisen soon gave way to the peaceful hillside and mountain views of the St Gallen district to the north-east,

but for once his beloved mountains could not provide the solace he wanted. His past had caught up
with him in a violent, destructive, and evil way.

From the moment that Stefan Weiss got into the car
with his young friends at the age of sixteen, the
downward spiral of life had begun. For that journey
took only a few minutes, leading to a park on the
east bank of Lake Zurich, but the effects were to last
a lifetime. The youngsters gathered in the park they
nicknamed 'UFO landing-place', sitting on a bench
while one of the group produced a carved white clay
pipe from his pocket. A plastic bag came from
another pocket and was handed to another of the
group who held it carefully while a third member
produced tobacco. Delicately he tipped some
tobacco into the bowl of the pipe while another
rubbed at the block of rubber-like substance that
had come from the plastic bag. Fragments mingled
with the tobacco.

When the bowl was full the first youngster raised
the pipe to his lips—the grinning head carved
round the bowl looking almost contemptuously
around—and struck a match. They closed round
the flame to keep it alight until the tobacco glowed
red. Then they watched, almost in awe, as their
leader took a few puffs and passed the pipe along
the row, each boy puffing in turns. Stefan, excitement throbbing in his chest, sucked deeply, managed to avoid the temptation to cough and let
himself down, and passed the pipe on. The hash
mingled with the tobacco and gave it a pleasant,
heady taste. At first as he sensed the drug filtering
through his system he felt proud; months of watch-

ing his friends, knowing what they were doing, but too shy to ask to be invited to participate, had been rewarded.

When the last embers had been sucked from the pipe the boisterous group made their way into a café alongside the park, but as they drank and ate Stefan felt waves of nausea sweep over him. He stumbled from the café and made for the bench, lying down and feeling the effects of the drug work through him. His head felt dizzy and light all at the same time, drifting above him. Cautious as he had been when smoking the pipe, peeping at the few visitors to ensure that none knew him, he was now uncaring; willing to face the world while the influence of his first session with drugs lasted.

Eyes reddened by the drug made him careful to creep into his house later on without his parents hearing him. Father was perched, as usual, at the lounge table, the surface smothered in papers and books, his briefcase lying half-open on the floor. It seemed to Stefan that, since his father had become a bank director, every evening merely meant more work, catching up with the events of the day and getting ahead of the next—probably necessary if the family were to keep up standards expected of them, since moving to the Meilen district alongside the lake (named the gold-coast by jealous working classes).

He was also to need the money to make up the shortfall in Stefan's education. Missing out on grammar school because of his lack of results, Stefan was later sent to a private commercial college in Zurich in an attempt to encourage him to follow in the businesslike footsteps of his father and grandfather.

For the 16-year-old life at the commercial college—Juventus Schulen—was interesting, but
more for the extra-mural activities than what went
on in the classroom. The dull, serried ranks of
windows in the walls of the commercial college had
more to offer than the noisy outlook over the shunt-
ing yards alongside Zurich's railway station. They
also offered the excitement of new friends—an
extrovert crowd who wandered the corridors of the
school barefoot, wore ear-rings and dangled
bangles from their wrists. The two-year course,
including English, French and German, commercial maths, business studies, bookkeeping, short-
hand and typing, and economics, appealed to
Stefan but he found too many distractions which
deflected his mind from the studious pathway it
should have been following.

He had few friends and all his young life had
been spent creating a strong friendship with one
individual only to call it off at the slightest difference of opinion to slip into another one-person
relationship. All long-haired, cheekily confident,
spontaneous and always ready to confront the lecturers, this latest selection from which to choose a
friend was enticing. He chose Martin, a lad intent
on enjoying life to the full—and ignoring college if
it prevented that enjoyment. Their lunch-times
were spent roaming the nearby streets of the city,
inevitably ending up at the station with its under-
ground warren of little shops and passageways.

It was there that Stefan found himself introduced
and then dragged further into a twilight world of
corruption that was to cost him dear. He spotted a
tall, middle-aged, well-dressed man following him

one day. For some reason he couldn't explain Stefan turned the tables and followed the man as well. When they lost each other he couldn't understand what he had been doing. Later, when in the men's toilet underneath the station, the empty cavern suddenly became the stage for a group of men giggling and winking at him as he stood against the urinal. Days later, in a conversation with his close friend, the two elements were put together. To Stefan homosexuals had merely been misguided men who were the butt of childish humour. Now he began to show an interest.

One day he agreed to go with his friend and discover how much money was to be made from their youthful bodies. Waiting under the towering dull brick arches at the rear of the station they saw the men wandering around, staring as if weighing up the attraction of the male drivers who unloaded passengers.

Eventually a car pulled up alongside them and a man invited them to join him. They looked at each other, nodded in unison, and climbed into the back of the car. They were to return some minutes later having satisfied the man and lined their pockets with a hundred francs. Stefan's friend was excited at the money they had made so easily. Stefan was just as intrigued by the incident itself.

He didn't feel repulsed, dirty or sullied; simply strangely stirred emotionally. For some weeks the couple shared the money they made from homosexual activities, but then Stefan decided to go alone. Young-looking for his sixteen years, he had begun to realise that while he was enjoying the experiences with other men his friend was merely grasping at the money. And Stefan, a good-looking youngster, intuitively knew he could make more of that on his own.

He was also well aware that the friend could not control his tongue, and Stefan was afraid that if he continued working with him everyone at school and ultimately home would know what he was doing.

In a strange way he wasn't ashamed of it: but recognised that others would not understand. He met another friend—a man of about thirty, Pius— who gave him another thing he wanted, a father-figure. Stefan had begun to realise that deep in his heart he wanted an elder man to look up to, some-thing lacking in his relationship with his own father. Pius provided that something.

He lived in a flat near the city centre so their sexual activity took place there—often during the weekends when Stefan's parents assumed he was staying with friends from college.

For six years it was to be a friendship that stuck, although Stefan still satisfied an increasing desire to be with other men, and the need for money, by continuing as a male prostitute to a regular clientele of men with whom he felt safe and who paid well for his youthful service.

In a week he could have earned 3,000 francs. In fact he never did because much of his free time was spent with Pius who, because of his special friend-ship, was never charged; providing instead the love, affection and security the young man wanted. Any money Stefan did earn was spent on another of his increasing addictions—drugs.

Experiments with hash had led him to buy his own set of pipes to smoke the drug and then, with the encouragement of friends, to taste the dubious pleasures of hashish, LSD and other easy-to-obtain drugs. Sniffing typewriter-cleaning fluid poured freely into a paper bag, which he had also tried, now seemed tame by comparison.

At the college, teachers—some hardly older than the pupils they were educating—warned the students about the dangers of drugs but that only served to whet Stefan's appetite and sharpen his desires. It was a short cut to popularity. Always shy and afraid to push his way to the front, Stefan badly wanted to be accepted and admired by the long-haired rebels he trailed. Even his pipe-smoking hash adventures were tame compared with the marijuana he moved on to, and the regular supply of tablets he was taking.

The riverside walk, a short distance from the station, became his new adventure playground—the so-called Riviera walk where youngsters sat in ranks up the stone steps leading to the water and drug pedlars plied their dangerous trade. Stefan had become an old hand at checking the weight of the block of hash in a plastic package, or instantly knowing the quality of the dried-looking marijuana leaves, which were rubbed and simply folded into cigarette paper to be smoked and usher him into another dreamy, distant world.

School was a problem for the youngster desperate for drugs and homosexual activity. The neon lights that pounded light into the gloomy classrooms merely emphasised the bright lights that waited for him at the rear of the station or in the comfort of Pius's flat. But he also wanted the diploma which went with the studies. The two-year course had almost ended when things got on top of Stefan and he walked out, preferring to hitch-hike to the south of France and taste the winter air by the coast. The principal told him not to return, but relented after approaches from Stefan's parents and agreed to take the boy back—although he had to repeat the whole of his second year.

The year dragged on with Stefan eventually getting the diploma. The college diploma, however, was unrecognised outside the school, and so he had to agree to spend an extra year working in a company while studying in the evenings and weekends to gain a national diploma which would be recognised by most commercial companies in Switzerland.

Stefan began working for an insurance company as a junior clerk, moving through departments to learn the different aspects of the system, before he decided that the lure of travel and excitement was greater than regular employment and the possibility of the diploma. He walked out. The habit which was to dog his steps for much of his life, an inability to stick at anything, had surfaced yet again.

Weeks later he was called up and the Swiss army found themselves victims of Stefan's wanderlust. He was supposed to do seventeen weeks basic training but after only seventeen days demanded to see the camp psychologist and confessed to being a homosexual in a successful effort to get his service cut short. It was an interview which was reported by the authorities back to his parents—the first time that whatever suspicions they had about their son had actually been confirmed.

Stefan had even created a façade with his sex life, having a number of girl-friends whom he cared for and allowed to mother him, to provide what he considered to be another missing ingredient in his life. If the girls knew of his homosexual inclinations they rarely mentioned it. And certainly Stefan would not dream of confessing his relationships with women to his homosexual companions, except Pius whom he trusted as a father-figure.

His sex life in growing disarray on one hand, he was also holding the reins on a growing consumption of drugs. Hash and tablet drugs were now regular daily habits with worse to come.

The lack of consistency in his working life continued as he moved from job to job—each one becoming more menial than its predecessor. The few weeks when he had worked in the Migros supermarket chain's biscuit factory, watching the conveyor belt and feeding dough into machines to earn 800 francs to buy his first twelve-string guitar, had tainted him for life, it seemed. A negative impression of work had been implanted in his young mind that was to stay throughout his working days.

One of the few things he enjoyed regularly were the visits to the family holiday home in a popular central skiing district. As work became more irregular he began to stay on at the holiday home when his parents had taken him there. One Christmas he was out of work and hung on for a few extra days.

Stefan had been smoking his hash before stumbling his way towards the town restaurant. As he wobbled uneasily in the entrance an attractive blond girl opened the door for him, waving him in first. 'It's a lovely day,' she commented, not realising he was in no fit condition to assess the weather.

He slung his coat on a chair and worked his way through the self-service barriers, selecting a black coffee and a cake. As he returned to the seat he had so casually reserved it was to find the same girl sitting opposite him. There was instant magnetism between the pair, each one sensing in the person on the opposite side of the table a need and longing that was not being met. And both quickly guessed that the other was on drugs. Regina, who was staying with her parents at their holiday retreat, had arrived with her boy-friend, but he was soon ditched in favour of the more interesting Stefan. Stefan, embarrassed by his own popularity with such a good-looking girl, tried to apologise to the other man but was not entirely unhappy. Regina's blonde hair, close-clipped at the front, was allowed to hang long and loose at the back, and she wore Indian jewellery and a ready smile which entranced Stefan.

Their telepathic understanding and instant rapport kept her in his memory after he went back to Zurich. When his parents returned to the holiday lodge he telephoned Regina at her home in Basle, inviting her for a couple of days to Zurich, not expecting that she would come. She did, arriving the next day and immediately moving into his bed. In the affluent district of Zurich in which Stefan lived neighbours kept themselves to themselves and he knew their secret was safe. He discovered that Regina was using heroin—a habit he had often frowned on and refused to submit to. After sleeping together, however, he took Regina to a boisterous youth centre in the city where he knew he could buy the needs to satisfy her addiction.

When they returned to the house Regina wasn't the only one to plunge the needle of the syringe into her arm; Stefan took his first dose of heroin, the drug that was to speed his downward path.

The following weekend Stefan went to Basle and stayed with Regina, smiling at her parents' insistence that they sleep in separate rooms. When he had a noisy argument with his own parents later Stefan did not have to think what he would do: he simply packed a suitcase and took a train to Basle and Regina.

Three weeks later he had found a flat in the city and it wasn't long before an argument at her house caused her to move in with him. He had jobs—a laundry and then a store—but couldn't earn enough to satisfy the craving for heroin which became as great in him after a short time as it was in Regina. She got money by begging from friends and never repaying the loans. He began stealing from the till, or retaining credit cards, if customers were forgetful after making a purchase, and using the cards to buy goods which he could sell.

Life with Regina was at opposite extremes: he enjoyed himself both with her and with the occasional men he met for money. But his health was getting worse. A visit to the local hospital for what appeared to be jaundice led to Regina's parents discovering that he too was on heroin, but despite their pleas the couple continued with their lives in their own way. Even the warning from a local doctor that if he continued acting the way he was he would be lucky to live for another year didn't restrain Stefan.

Regina's parents wanted the couple to begin some sort of therapy to get them off drugs, and booked them into a counselling session. Stefan accompanied Regina, desperate for drugs but having no money until the following pay-day—and feeling that the counsellor, Reinhard Dettwiler, was someone who would probably help. He had intended to sit with Regina in the counselling room, only to find that they were seen separately. Instead he waited outside reading a red-covered Bible that had been given to her by her parents—Christians who had amazed him by praying over meals and speaking about God. It struck him as a book that wasn't very interesting.

Then he was called before the counsellor—a portly elderly man with streaks of white hair, and soft but serious eyes into which Stefan discovered he could not look. The counsellor, with no idea of Stefan's past, provided no medication but instead warned him about wasting his life on drugs and sex and insisted on praying with him. Stefan knelt awkwardly on the floor as the elderly man struggled down alongside him. Reinhard prayed while Stefan felt perspiration seeping down his face and the need for drugs increasing in his body. He stumbled a few words of prayer and made a hurried and welcome exit.

What conversations Stefan had had about his drug habit with medical authorities had convinced him, if he needed convincing, that he had to make some effort to stop. He had agreed to go to the Mannedorf Hospital, a regional hospital run by Christian nuns, to dry out, and they had insisted that he followed it by rehabilitation at a place called Best Hope, in the St Gallen area north-east of Zurich, where staff specialised in helping addicts.

Stefan had hardly entered the hospital when, in his desperate state, he began to demand drugs from a doctor. When they were refused it took five people to restrain Stefan, tying him to his bed where his harrowing treatment began. Dizzy and weak from medication his days drifted by. The Bible, which for some reason he had retained, lay on his bedside cubicle and a nurse began to talk to him about it. Obviously curious as to why anyone with a Bible should be a heroin-addict, she talked of Jesus Christ and her love for him and what he had done for her. The words swept over Stefan in an unintelligible murmur, but the love and concern for him as an individual which radiated from her face began to speak to him instead. Antje, dark-haired, and always wearing the white uniform, also told him about Best Hope and that he could be helped there.

Stefan wasn't so sure. Could anywhere help him? Did he even want help? Antje plied him with cassettes of sermons and booklets on Christian topics. He read and listened with increasing interest. All his life Stefan had been searching for something— truth . . . love . . . affection . . .—in a search that had sent him to bed with men and women, had filled his body with drugs and alcohol, could Best Hope help? Was the very name, chosen during a period when new places in Switzerland seemed always to take English names, an omen for good? Antje posed a question to Stefan in one of her talks about Jesus. Explaining that Jesus had promised to come back to the earth and take Christians—those who loved him—back to heaven with him, she asked: 'Would you go? If Jesus came back today what would happen to you?' Stefan considered the question as he lay awake that night. He had tried everything he knew; drugs, men, women and alcohol, but it had only succeeded in putting him into the hospital with a future that was questionable.

Marcel, a former drug-addict now at Best Hope, convinced him it could work. The one-time addict, tall, strong and well-built, was an Arab sent by the centre to tell Stefan how much Best Hope had helped him. 'If you go and make up your mind to think about Jesus and give up your old ways it can do the same for you,' he smiled. Because Marcel knew the traumas he was going through and could see through his own lies and excuses, Stefan was inclined to believe him.

He also knew that the doctor's warning that if he didn't mend his ways he would not see the year out was no idle threat: Best Hope could be his only hope. If it didn't work, he convinced himself, he would simply commit suicide!

Stefan began to read the red-covered Bible by his bedside and listen to the Christian cassettes with renewed interest; he was impressed as he was reading Mark's Gospel with the miracles that Jesus had performed—but could one happen to him? That was what was needed.

Within days he was to doubt. For his release from hospital meant he had to report to the police station to answer charges of theft and forging the credit cards—they had caught up with him at last, although in the end he was only given a sixteen-month suspended sentence because by the time his case came up, he was already at Best Hope. That pressure, on top of the fact that he was told he would have to wait six weeks before he could begin treatment at Best Hope, was too much. Soon he had found his way to the station and the drug dealers. In another effort to completely free himself from drugs, he agreed to go to a Christian retreat house run by the Blue Cross at Nesslau, Toggenburg, an hour from Zurich, for a month, during which time he managed to be more relaxed and exist on medication rather than the drugs which he would otherwise have sought.

From there his mother took him to Best Hope, an hour's drive from Zurich into the green hills near St Gallen. The car swung round a hairpin bend on a steep slope and the white sign with its black words struck him—Best Hope. It was his only hope. But would it work?

Apprehensively he examined the stately building with the twin circular towers on either side of the entrance, as the car pulled up the hill. The cream and red bricks gave it an impressive appearance which was emphasised as he pushed open the wooden, glass-panelled door leading into the lobby. He scuffed his shoes on the carpet and gingerly walked up the stone steps through two more doors into the entrance hall—a large inviting area suddenly filled with the advancing Hanspeter Vogt, whose vision the centre had been years before, striding towards him, hand outstretched. The warm greetings were received with mixed feelings by Stefan's mother, who was disappointed that the centre had religious connotations.

Stefan was taken to the office for a talk with Hanspeter and his wife, Anita, and made to take off the bangles, rings and ear-rings which for so long had marked his attempts to be different. Anita also went through his suitcase and removed some of his more outlandish clothing for his mother to take away with her. 'You won't need these,' she said with a grin.

Stefan's mother returned home later, satisfied at least that her son had reached his destination. A cure would now be up to him.

The building had originally been erected as a religious centre many years before by a group who believed that no room should be too square. For that reason all the ceilings were curved in attractive shapes and the rooms, overlooking green hillsides at the front and forest on the back, were pleasantly decorated. Stefan was taken to a room on one side of the building, looking out on to the pine trees of a small forest. His room-mate was Roland, a tall gangling man who insisted on praying together on their first evening and introducing Stefan to the necessity of daily Bible reading. Stefan, feeling awkward, knelt while Roland prayed and then lay in his bed contemplating his future, considering the struggles he sensed were ahead and whether he would ultimately return to the drug scene he knew so well.

Stefan began to slip into the Best Hope ritual of morning worship-times; singing hymns, praying and reading the Bible, followed by sessions of work—he was put in a carpentry team shaping wooden pot-stands, furniture and other items— with recreation such as football, volleyball and ice-skating. They also spent a couple of hours together in a sauna on Saturday afternoons—'it gives us time to talk without any stress,' pointed out Hanspeter.

A week or so after his arrival Stefan was driven home by Hanspeter to discard more unwanted items of luggage—photographs and clothing—but used the opportunity to grab a packet of tablets from his room as he did so. Later that night after returning to Best Hope he took them all, washing them down with water. As they began to take effect the weeks of being drug-free seemed to increase their power; he was wafted into a daze, eventually feeling someone was after him and racing off into the forest alongside the house. Rushing through the trees he was oblivious to the branches that flapped across his face, scratching him, and the brambles that tore at his legs as he hurtled between trees, desperate to escape the clutches of whatever it was that followed him. Finally, gasping for breath and sobbing with fear he made his way back to the centre and, finding his way into the darkened kitchen, flicked on the light. He grabbed a kitchen knife and began to slash at his wrists, anxious to end his troubles once and for all. Somehow he couldn't complete the task he had set himself. Blood oozed from the cuts across his arms, but the vital arteries had been protected from his assault.

Upstairs he persuaded Roland to bandage the wounds and say nothing. 'I'm better now,' he promised. 'I've asked God to forgive me and won't do it again.' Next morning he wore a shirt with the longest sleeves he had, in an effort to hide the bandages at breakfast and during the morning meeting. But he was called out of the service by Hanspeter, disappointed by his latest charge's obvious lack of willingness to co-operate. Confronted by the leader, Stefan said he no longer wanted to stay at Best Hope. 'In that case, telephone your parents and ask them to collect you.

There is nothing we can do for you. You must want to get well,' he was told.

With his parents away on holiday, Stefan simply packed his bag and hitch-hiked to Zurich, determined to erase the experience at Best Hope from his mind in the only way he knew how: drugs! Taking one of the family cars he drove through the city to a friend for drugs, only to be refused. He had better luck with a dealer and immediately sent his mind soaring . . . He tried to walk about in the car, his head banging against the windscreen, as the drugs robbed him of his senses. The next thing he knew was waking up in a friend's house and discovering that he had been found on the doorstep, drugged, with 500 francs in his pocket. The car was later discovered, doors wide open, alongside a main street in the city. Stefan was never to remember the events of those few hours.

They led him, however, back to the Blue Cross Centre in Nesslau. Best Hope agreed to allow him to return providing he was off drugs. After withdrawal in the centre, he returned to his room at Best Hope, easing himself once more into the daily routine, dreading the daily question-and answer-sessions that constituted part of the therapy treatment.

He began to ask questions about the Bible—a book he couldn't understand. 'How could Jesus help all those people who had done nothing for him?' he puzzled. 'Why did he forgive those who killed him?' But the constant exposure to Christian influence began to soften the young man. He began to feel that God existed and was interested in him, personally.

But when that interest began to grow, another disaster struck. On a working holiday with a small group from the centre in the Italian-speaking part of Switzerland, he found his glands badly swollen; a fever sent his temperature soaring; he had chronic diarrhoea and the weight lost by his drug-taking, which he had been steadily restoring, began to disappear once more. In a terribly weakened state he had to stay in bed. A doctor checked him over with a puzzled expression, finally taking blood and other samples for testing.

Then he was sent to hospital for more tests. As he went from bad to worse he returned to hospital to meet with the chief officer in the hospital. It was then, in the compact office leading off the examination room, that Stefan was told 'not to worry, we'll soon find out what's wrong,' but at the same time saw the word AIDS on the medical report. He then knew what the score was.

Even though the doctor said nothing about it and although in 1983 AIDS was still very new, Stefan had read a few articles about the killer disease. Back at Best Hope he told Hanspeter, who called the team together to pray for him. He was given his own room and his own utensils and crockery and was instructed to wash them himself after meals. In spite of living somewhat in isolation, he always felt accepted.

Further tests showed that he had toxoplasmosis, which could have caused some of the effects similar to AIDS such as the fever, loss of weight, and glandular swelling. The doctors were keen to avoid labelling him an AIDS victim so early in the medical history of the disease. They checked spinal fluid, and a gland. His blood, they discovered, was susceptible to infection; it had little ability to resist.

But the problem was that the effects dragged on—for a period of time far longer than was common in toxoplasmosis. On the other hand, in cases in which AIDS-related complex was diagnosed, the individuals involved invariably went on to develop AIDS itself eventually. The medical profession lacked the tests which were to be invented within a few years to test for AIDS.

A different doctor told him: 'Because you have completely changed your life-style and are not having sexual contact with men or women, and do not now take drugs, there is a good chance you can recover.' Stefan wanted to know exactly what he had and forced the issue. 'I saw the word AIDS on my report. Do I have it?' he demanded.

The doctor admitted that there was a 95 per cent chance he had, and they were afraid that soon the more virulent symptoms of the Human Immunodeficiency Virus infection might show themselves— brain infection, various forms of cancer and other illnesses taking over as his inability to combat even the smallest sickness was exposed.

Talks with Hanspeter at Best Hope led the doctor to ask if they would take Stefan back 'to help him enjoy his remaining time in peace'.

Restless and afraid of the thought of death, Stefan considered all he had heard of Jesus and heaven and couldn't get too excited about that prospect either—if he was bound for heaven. It was then that Reinhard Dettwiler, who had counselled him some years before, arrived at the centre for what, unknown to Stefan, was a regular counselling day when all the participants at Best Hope could speak to him. When he saw Stefan he remembered their previous conversation and, with no prior knowledge of his diagnosis, told him: 'You need to be born again. At present you are like the thief on the cross hanging alongside Jesus at his death—you are in trouble and know it, and simply want Jesus to help you get out of trouble. But to do so you have to ask him into your life, to forgive every area of your life. You have to give yourself completely to God and allow him to rule your actions.

'You must clean up your life—otherwise you will die.'

Stefan, who had known the mechanics of being a Christian for many months and had copied the habits of those around him to increasing perfection, suddenly realised that the old man was speaking the truth. There was more to Christianity than pretending: it had to be real—and he had to be real before God.

Stefan was sent home for a few days to think it through. 'We want to make sure that you can conquer the past through the power of Christ,' said Hanspeter. And the sick man knew that he needed to be broken, but recognised he couldn't break himself. He returned to Best Hope days later to tell Hanspeter he was convinced that Christ was his only answer. He confessed that he had had a homosexual life-style before going to Best Hope and that he had considered it simply a normal part of life—something all men felt. As he confessed his past and asked for forgiveness, Stefan felt the tension within him drain away. He knew that he was a Christian. He knew that if Christ returned now he would be ready.

Months followed of steady progress, fighting to control his thought-life: 'It's like being an alcoholic,' he said to one friend. 'Once an alcoholic—always an alcoholic. You simply have to steer clear of the first drink. I must keep clear of drugs, and I have to make an effort to control my thoughts where men are concerned.'

Within days of his decision he noticed a marked improvement; the temperature receded and the swollen glands reduced. He began to gain weight again.

For Stefan the battle with the past was over. Christ had won. Two years after that initial suspected diagnosis his blood was tested again—HIV-AIDS positive. The sample taken on the earlier occasion was also tested using new methods—that too was AIDS positive. Stefan was a carrier of the virus, infected for the rest of his life and potentially infectious to others who came into contact with him sexually or with his blood.

Had it been the beginning of the actual AIDS epidemic in 1981, medical opinion would have expected him to invariably show the later stages of AIDS and to die within a year or two. So far, apart from being a carrier and more susceptible than most people to colds and flu, Stefan is able to live a normal life.

Months after finishing his course at Best Hope he managed to get a job in a bank but was sacked when they discovered he was HIV-AIDS positive. He then discovered his present job—working for the Heli Mission, a Swiss Christian company using helicopters to help bring aid of a different kind to Third World countries.

His one-time girl-friend Regina has been given only months to live. She has AIDS. Many of Stefan's friends have died or been given similar sentences. Internationally, it is said, ten million people in a hundred and thirty countries may be suffering from what has been referred to as the twentieth-century plague.

Neither Stefan, his friends, nor the doctors take it for granted that his present good physical condition is permanent. Through his confrontation with the disease his inward and outward life has been lastingly changed.

He knows that he ought not to have children should he get married, and that he will never be able to safely enjoy the sexual side of married life to the full without adequate protection. 'But,' he told a Christian conference, 'However long I live, even if it is cut short by AIDS, I am determined to live for Jesus. He has given me a whole new life—I want it to be worthwhile.'

6

Maeve: Chased by depression

The sun and sand of Puerto Rico and the hectic social whirl should have been enough to encourage Maeve O'Reilly to enjoy life to the full. Instead it served only to reinforce the loneliness she felt inside. For the 25-year-old Aer Lingus worker could never shake off the feeling that she was constantly missing something—even on holiday.

It had been the same ever since she first entered the crew control department of the bustling air terminal alongside Dublin airport when she was nineteen. The gold braid of the pilots and the smart green-blue suits of the hostesses couldn't lure her from the desk job she enjoyed. Shielded by filing cabinets and a large desk from the remainder of the noisy open-plan operations department, she loved the pressure of making sure that flight crews left on time, and the surge of adrenalin when a crew was late from a previous flight and had to be substituted, after making certain that the replacement crew had sufficient rest time and were not likely to over-run their working hours during the switched flight.

Controlled by the Pilot's Association agreement and safety regulations, it was a pressured but exciting job. And it presented her with travel perks, such as the regular holidays in her favourite spot, Puerto Rico, in the guest house where airline personnel could stay reasonably cheaply.

In Dublin the social life was as hectic: drinks after work often preceding nights at dance-halls, or parties where the liquor flowed freely and her bouncy, chirpy Irish sense of humour always guaranteed her plenty of friends.

But still there was an emptiness, and a sense of loneliness that always nagged away at the back of Maeve's mind. Life was full—but it wasn't satisfying. She didn't seem to fit in anywhere. 'It always seems as if everyone else is having a good time but I don't even feel I'm there. The things they do seem pointless,' she confided to a close friend on one occasion. On other, but rarer, moments, she sought solace in the confessional box of the nearest Roman Catholic church, glad of the protection provided by the carved screen which cut her off from the priest and through which she whispered her words of confession.

Life for Maeve had always seemed to be like that. Born in Dublin in 1941, church was always a duty—father insisted the family went to Mass on Sunday but religion didn't interfere with family life other than that weekly procession. Even in the convent school where she was sent, the religious activities became just another part of the educational system and meaningless outside of it.

Her career as a pharmacist was short-lived, the apprenticeship ending with the death of her father when she was only eighteen months into the course, and financial need pushing her out to find her job with Aer Lingus, a more lucrative response to family necessity.

She soon slipped into the system alongside the other four girls in the department, shuffling through the different shifts and discovering how to handle people as she faced irate pilots anxious to demand their rights, and tried not to overburden the more amenable ones who were friendly and willing.

Maeve's career-girl appearance often belied her feelings which longed for marriage and the security and stability offered by a husband. Then, she considered, the constant feeling of loneliness would leave her. She had almost been engaged at seventeen but the suitor had emigrated to America, and despite letters begging her to join him, Maeve decided that distance didn't lend enchantment. She had met him near her home—his father was a chauffeur at the American Embassy, which was near the semi-detached house alongside Phoenix Park in which Maeve lived with her parents, two older brothers and younger sister.

She had not had a particularly happy childhood with her father, an austere man who had carried his army background into family life, even when he worked in the Aer Lingus customs clearance department. Years later she had stood at his hospital bedside as he lay dying and recalled the only one occasion she had felt close: a weekend on which he had taken her to London as a 12-year-old and they had almost been like friends, talking and enjoying the sights. As soon as they returned to Dublin, however, his taciturn nature had returned as if they had never been away at all.

Hockey was one of the activities which Maeve did enjoy at school, and at which she excelled; though she had not been quite good enough to win a place in the Irish junior international squad. Playing for Malahide, near the airport, she was captain of the team and was once invited to take part in an Irish junior trial but it turned out to be a disaster. She was the only player from her club in the trial whereas most of the other girls were in twos and threes, and it showed when the game got under way. The match was the opposite of playing in her own team—everyone was out to make individual points and Maeve, the solo girl on the wing, hardly saw the ball.

Maeve also turned out for the Aer Lingus side and a mixed team, Loraine, with the odd weekend tournament taking her to London and Frankfurt on occasions. And always there was the social drinking after the matches.

Apparently happy-go-lucky and always first on the list for parties, Maeve was very mixed up inside. She desperately wanted someone with whom to share her feelings and emotions but a brief involvement with a pilot who was married left her devastated and lonelier than ever.

It was not, in fact, until Maeve agreed, reluctantly, to go with her mother to the wedding of friends in London that she did meet a man who promised more than simply one-night stands. Unfortunately—or fortunately for Maeve—she was delayed on a skiing holiday in Austria and returned the day after the wedding. But when she telephoned her mother from the flat of a friend in London to apologise she was invited across London to meet the relatives—and the bridal couple who were not yet on honeymoon.

Maeve was told to wait at the flat until the best man arrived to collect her. Tony George was about her height—just over five feet—blond, and with a pleasant personality. His good looks and soft Birmingham accent appealed to Maeve as they chatted during the drive through the northern tip of the city.

A designer in a heating and ventilating services company, Tony was an interesting character, probably because his life-style was so different from that of Maeve. He was an oasis in the middle of a boring desert of a day. Later he drove her back and the pair made tentative arrangements to meet next time she was in London.

That occasion was a month away, but as Maeve waited for Tony on the Friday evening she got angrier by the minute: he failed to turn up. The following day he finally arrived—apologising because he had been made redundant without warning and to make matters worse a concrete garage had collapsed on the car, which did indeed bear the imprint of his story. The same afternoon, in fact, he had to visit the friend of a relative and was offered a job looking after a camp-site in North Wales.

A few weeks later Maeve visited him on the site—a disastrous weekend! Cold and damp, she was made by the site-owner to stay in a chilly caravan while Tony lived in the warm, protected house. The presence of Tony's cheerful parents took some of the tension from the weekend and Maeve agreed to visit them in Birmingham when she was next free.

In fact the relationship blossomed and continued. Tony eventually ditched the camp-site job in favour of his old heating and ventilating field. His warm, friendly family gave Maeve what she felt she had never had—love and attention—and she even enjoyed the regular weekly trips to visit her aunt and grandmother.

The couple had met in January, were engaged on Christmas Day that same year and married ten months later at the small chapel in Dublin Airport. The young Roman Catholic priest had no objections to marrying a Catholic to a Protestant and succeeded in getting a dispensation from the bishop, while the airport chapel ceremony appealed to the 27-year-old bride's sense of occasion. The honeymoon was in Beirut, Lebanon, where the couple enjoyed the luxurious beaches and noisy markets, and Tony tried to overcome his natural shyness at making his first trip abroad.

Married life in Birmingham was very different for Maeve. The couple bought their own semi-detached house in Harborne and after some months of boredom Maeve got a job in a bank. That lasted only weeks, before she snapped up an offer from the Birmingham office of Aer Lingus only to discover it lacked the variety and excitement of her airport-based work. Now she was office-bound but juggling only with reservations and business problems.

One thing both had decided: no children. It was when an unusually sombre Tony had suddenly asked her about the Pope's statement opposing birth control that Maeve burst out laughing, and said, 'What's it got to do with him?' and their unwritten agreement not to have children had been made.

For Maeve life ought to have been satisfying. She had her own little white sports car—an MG Midget—a home, a husband, and a well-paid job. But despite her feelings of years before, that marriage would change her, she sensed it hadn't. That very knowledge brought the black clouds of depression with greater regularity. Even though she enjoyed Tony's family, the constant ritual visits to relatives and the nearness of everyone began to annoy her.

Satisfaction always seemed to elude her. When she found her work was too straightforward she switched departments to discover that that too became boring. Doctors could do little other than prescribe tablets to help her relax. She began to take them. For a few weeks they worked and sta bilised her long enough to enjoy a few weeks more of tension-free life but gradually, very gradually, the times between taking drugs began to reduce.

Another job brought fresh challenge. She was taken on to organise the summer schools for the Open University in its first year of such a venture from Birmingham. Maeve jumped at it, booking Keele University in Staffordshire for a few hundred students the first year, and watching her arrangements tick along with clockwork precision. She booked tutors, professors, and accommodation in the university campus.

But the second year brought more pressures, and despite her organising ability Maeve would not learn to delegate. She shouldered even more duties as the student numbers were swollen by a fresh intake, and she popped more pills into her mouth with greater regularity to keep on top of the headaches, depression and mental strain.

Maeve moved into Keele to prepare the university and make the final arrangements. For a week she slogged away juggling with rooms, accommodation and a timetable for the thousand or so students and lecturers. She then spent a hectic day welcoming the visitors, signing them in, and instructing them in the timetable.

Late that evening she flung herself on the small single bed in the spartan university accommodation. It hardly seemed that she had slept before she was awake. Her head ached, buzzing and singing. She didn't know where she was. Yanking aside the curtains she saw, perched in front of the building, the familiar sight of her little white car parked on the shingle drive. Feeling her mind snap Maeve grabbed clothing, stuffed it into the fibre-glass brown suitcase and rushed from the room, hurtling down the stairs and crashing the door behind her as she burst into the sultry July early-morning air.

As she pressed her right foot on the accelerator and watched the speedometer creep up, her muddled mind could only think of Tony: not the easygoing husband who always seemed able to calm her when her nerves were at bursting point, but a husband who might be having an affair with another woman. She imagined his assistant, an attractive, dark-haired girl, sleeping in her bed. The thought tantalised her as she roared through the dawn in the confines of the sports car.

Slamming on the brakes outside the door of their home she rammed a key in the lock and hurtled inside and up the stairs, to find Tony peering blearily from the blankets, alone and puzzled. Maeve burst into tears and flung herself on the bed sobbing hysterically.

Tony telephoned Keele later that morning and told the officials that Maeve would not be back. Then he took a cup of tea to Maeve and began to soothe her frayed nerves. It was a Sunday morning, so they decided she would visit the doctor the following morning. For three months she was off work, existing for some time on tranquillisers until life seemed to return to some semblance of normality.

Maeve's flair for always being able to get a challenging job was fulfilled as soon as she felt fit, and she walked into the Queen Elizabeth Medical Centre to get a management job in the laboratories' department. She was in charge of the computer processing unit for the laboratories—irrespective of the fact that she couldn't even type!

Unafraid of a new challenge, it provided the stimulus her brain needed for a time, the occasional drug only needed for peak periods of pressure. After four years the transfer of work from an ageing computer system to a new one was completed and Maeve looked for a fresh challenge, finding it in a new job as assistant administrator in the Birmingham Maternity Hospital.

As far as her career went Maeve had reached the top. She had a top administrative position—without the qualifications!—a good home and husband, and had managed to keep her depressive elements subdued for the most part for the four years since her breakdown at Keele.

The new job gave her the adrenalin-inspired
energy she needed for a while longer before she was
forced to return to the doctor for increasing supplies
of tablets. Tony couldn't fail to notice the nervous
tension that was building up in his wife and took
steps to launch a new career for them both. His
work was intense and he was often called to work
late or spend long days away from home. The one
relaxation they both enjoyed was a boat they owned
on the Oxfordshire canal.

When they did escape for a weekend Tony and
his brother enjoyed tinkering with the boat's engine
and were often called on to rescue other boat
owners who had trouble. The plan they conceived
was to live on a boat and provide a water-borne
rescue service, like the RAC, for boat owners. They
also managed to agree a deal with a marina in
Fenny Compton, Warwickshire, in which they
would take over the maintenance and booking
administration for a fleet of hire boats.

Their house was sold and a purpose-built old-
style hand-painted narrow boat bought as their
home. But as Maeve stood at the tiller steering the
colourful boat towards their new berth on a chilly
October day it was more than the weather that
provided a cold prodding finger inside her. Without
the security of a house she didn't know whether she
could cope. Buster, a little Staffordshire bull terrier
to which she had become attached, suddenly
dashed from the boat and raced along a road. A
desperate Maeve and Tony couldn't find him anywhere. At the end of their search they pushed their
way into a pub to spot the little pet perched
alongside a table.

If Maeve was relieved she was having difficulty in showing it. Her face was taut and lined, already subject to the nervous tensions that kept her fingers wrapping round each other and her mind unable to sleep at night.

At Fenny Compton she saw another doctor, a young man who promised he had 'tablets for everything'. It was a trail Maeve was to find impossible to break. She began taking mixtures of medication and tablets—heavy duty tranquillisers—and from then on there would be no time that she was free from medication of some sort.

Tony was now resigned to her state. Life progressed. For two or three months a new combination of drugs would lift Maeve's spirits sufficiently for her to manage her work—that, and the increasing reliance on the vodka bottle that was now beginning to be a companion in the evenings on her long-boat home. Always she lived with the knowledge that her mind seemed to be cracking up. It seemed to be only a hair's breadth away from bursting point.

Squash and hockey failed to push back the increasing reliance on drugs and the desperate feeling of inadequacy. Maeve began to hate meeting people, detesting her duties in the office on the days when she had to introduce new customers to their boats and show them round.

Even in her distant, befuddled, state Maeve sensed that something was happening to her relationship with Tony. He had always had a comforting nature—one of the reasons his secretary, assistant and various others had confided in him in his previous job—but now she observed a woman from another boat company was telephoning him regularly and it always seemed to be Tony who went when she needed help.

One Sunday evening Maeve and Tony were relaxing in their boat when the telephone rang. Tony answered it and quickly moved a hand as if to hide his whispers. It was obviously the other woman. Maeve seethed with anger. Hurt, she challenged him when the phone was finally returned to its cradle but he refused to talk. For the first time she sensed a coldness in his attitude. After a night with hardly any sleep Maeve was up early packing her suitcase. Tony seemed upset but obviously thought she was bluffing. But when he went to the office Maeve slung the case in the boot of the silver Mercedes they now owned and drove off.

Despite the bursting in her mind, which flickered and seemed to refuse to halt on any one subject, she managed to get to their bank in Birmingham, take out £2,000 and open a new account in her own name. Then she drove for hours in ever-increasing circles, eventually stopping at some bed-and-breakfast place. Her nervousness was heightened by the over-friendly proprietor who quizzed her. 'Where are you going? Where have you been? How long will you be staying?' Maeve had no answers. To escape more questions she left the cottage and drove until she found a pub, bought a bottle of wine to take back to her room, only to discover she couldn't recall where the cottage was. She drove around desperately and finally, in utter frustration, stopped outside a police station where they managed to discover where her accommodation was and accompanied her back.

Next morning she left for the anonymity of a hotel in Warwick. She telephoned Tony who was distraught. He had called everyone he could think of but to no effect. He went immediately to the hotel to see her and suggested she go and stay with his mother for a while (his father having died some years earlier). There was no affair, he promised. The woman was simply a sympathetic listener.

Two weeks later he was to change his mind and tell Maeve there was someone else and that their marriage was over. Maeve had decided to return to the boat to pick up some more belongings and her heart sank as she opened the door and saw shoes and clothing spread around its normally spotless interior. They belonged, she could tell, to children. Then she investigated the bedroom, only to see the other woman's nightclothes and the small dressing table smothered in someone else's perfume and powder bottles. There was an unpleasant encounter with Tony who returned before Maeve had packed all her things, but she stormed off—never to return.

Tablets kept her from going under completely and Maeve returned to Dublin to consider her future. With nothing to keep her in Birmingham and, as she discovered, little to hold her in Dublin, she called a friend in Australia who had often asked her to visit. Even as the Qantas Jumbo touched down at Sydney, Maeve sensed she had done the wrong thing again. A mental wreck, she demonstrated quickly to her friend, Gabrielle, and her husband, that she was a liability. Gabrielle managed to take Maeve to a psychiatrist but she could not conquer her drinking and reliance on drugs. She refused meals with the family and existed on cheese and apples in her own room until Gabrielle could stand it no longer. Because Maeve's air ticket was a return and dated some weeks away Gabrielle and her husband bought her ticket to London and put her on a plane for Heathrow, afterwards telephoning Maeve's sister, Geraldine, in Dublin to tell her: 'We've put Maeve on the plane to England. She's in a terrible condition and needs a lot of help. There's nothing we can do for her.'

Geraldine flew to London and was at the airport to meet Maeve when she stumbled through the arrivals doors. The couple immediately flew on to Dublin to arrive a week before Christmas, with Maeve drugged and considering suicide because she felt no one cared. Taken into her sister's home Maeve discovered that her family and friends did their best to make Christmas a happy time for her. She responded, feeling that at last someone was interested and within days of the festivities finishing she was seeing a psychiatrist recommended by Geraldine.

A fresh round of treatment began, but again only the medication seemed to have any effect—and, once more, only for a limited period. A receptionist course gave her some incentive for a while and led to a new job, but it was one she was unable for once to control. Instead drugs, drink and depression controlled her. The boss, who tried to help her, decided to take on a girl part-time to help Maeve, and it was that appointment that was to have far-reaching effects.

For Marion began to befriend Maeve. They spent many lunch hours walking by the nearby canal and, as Marion talked, Maeve began to see something different in her. She sensed that Marion's interest was genuine, without wanting reward and without condemning Maeve for her condition. Marion passed on small leaflets for Maeve to read —they contained passages from the Bible—and she often talked about Christianity as a way to conquer life's problems. But Maeve, who had difficulty concentrating, found reading the leaflets was impossible and she listened politely to stories of other people who Marion knew had been helped by Christianity.

Maeve's nerves began to fray even more. She found it too difficult to cook a meal for herself each evening; work became a traumatic succession of enormous problems; and even making a cup of tea was such a major operation that it was easier to twist open a vodka bottle and have a drink.

It seemed better to attempt to blot out life and that's what she did, drinking vodka and taking drugs until it was impossible to work at all. Eventually Geraldine took her to the psychiatric unit at Blanchardstown Hospital and for three months Maeve suffered under the pressure of withdrawing into a shell of her own making, the small hospital room with its metal frame bed, locker and wardrobe becoming her world. Sleeping tablets sent her into a dreamy haze at night and during the day the staff had to force her to eat and tried to encourage her to face life. Telling Maeve that there was no more they could do for her the hospital officials sent her out.

For a week she lived with Geraldine until she found a flat in the house of an elderly lady. Marion had visited her occasionally at the hospital, sometimes taking her for a ride in her little minicar but she too found it impossible to break through the barrier that Maeve was building round herself.

In the new flat Maeve decided that she had only one option: suicide. On Sunday morning she drove herself to Howth Heath, a popular beauty spot, but discovered that because the cliff sloped outwards if she jumped over she would only hit the cliff and not the water. She decided against it. Then she considered a midnight trip to the sea—just walking out in the water until it swallowed up her problems. But again on the night she made her move the telephone rang, broke the spell, and she slumped in her chair with the vodka bottle instead.

She was supposed to be visiting a day centre for the mentally disturbed but that too was a traumatic effort. Maeve was frightened of going—and afraid not to go. The tension built to an unbearable pitch until her third attempt at suicide.

This time she merely rummaged around in the medicine cupboard and simply took every tablet she could find—128 she counted, of varied colours and shapes. She knew the elderly lady who owned the house was going on holiday early the next morning, so waited until she had gone and then, at six o'clock on the Saturday morning, put the tablets in her mouth and washed them down with water. Lying on the bed she drifted into a hazy sleep that she thought would herald death . . .

On Monday morning she woke. Her head ached. The bed was a mess of vomit. She was alive. That knowledge made her more dejected—she had failed again. Weak and dizzy she managed to telephone a friend from her Aer Lingus days, Mary, who was soon on hand to help. And another friend, who had been counselling Maeve, also arrived to tell her: 'You are very lucky. It was only because you took too many tablets that you are alive. They made you sick and that got them out of your system.'

Those words gave her the impetus to try again when she was alone—and to try with a more moderate dose of drugs. This time she took just ten—and woke again feeling as desperate as on the previous occasion. An air pistol, bought to keep on board the boat in the marina, came into her mind and she managed to get it from her belongings and snap back the barrel to insert a pellet into the dark interior. Putting the barrel against her temple she tensed and pulled the trigger. The weapon refused to fire. Another failure.

Going downhill fast she made her way to the one place she had always dreaded, St Brendan's mental hospital in Dublin. Somehow there semed no other place to go. Her belongings were taken from her: all except her nightclothes. Maeve was taken into an observation ward with ten beds, trying not to look as the eyes of the other nine inmates followed her sadly down the central passage. The room was permanently locked: staff were in attendance and others peered occasionally through the port-hole windows in the heavy duty doors. Maeve was accompanied everywhere by a nurse—even to the bath and toilet. Depressed and degraded she slunk to her bed for days on end—life was finished.

Five weeks later she was placed in a main ward and given occupational therapy—putting letters and other papers into envelopes for charity organisations. Even that was too much. Simply remembering that one of each of the three different coloured papers had to be folded together and slipped into the envelope was too incomprehensible to take in.

She wandered among the thirty or forty people in the ward, a long corridor-like room with small partitions on each side creating areas for eight people to sleep in. It was a mixture of young and old, and Maeve's fear grew as she studied the faces of those around her and saw how forgotten and seemingly worthless they had become. Her hands were constantly wringing, and there was the constant fear of a padded cell if she broke down and became violent as she saw some patients do.

Geraldine and one or two others visited her on occasions but it hardly seemed to matter. The doctors told Geraldine that her sister was unlikely ever to be able to go out and lead a normal life again. Life had ended—or so she thought.

For six weeks she was in the ward, gradually getting weaker, more depressed, losing every vestige of self-confidence—knowing it was happening and being unable to do anything about it.

But on the morning of 18 November 1982—her forty-first year—everything changed. There was no obvious reason for it. No warning it was to happen. No premonition. Maeve simply woke, and knew she was free. The fears, anxieties and dread that had greeted her each day for years had gone, to be replaced by hope. She knew she was cured. Maeve looked out of the window and the world looked different—the sky was blue, the trees a shimmering green, and even the lawns in the hospital grounds seemed to have a cheerful sparkle. She saw birds fluttering and heard their cheerful chirping. And as those instant sensations began to fill her mind and heart she knew something else: God had cured her.

It had to be him. It couldn't be anyone else. Everything else had failed—drugs, drink, doctors, friends, her own efforts. For years Maeve had known only her own problems—they had swamped her feelings—but now she was free of them and was aware of life and God.

The door creaked open and a voice called out: 'Does anyone want communion?' It was the priest whom Maeve had ignored for weeks. 'I do,' she responded. He stood at her bedside and asked her if she wanted to confess anything. Maeve did: her life spilled out in a torrent as she confessed how wicked she had been, particularly to attempt to take her own life. But this time she was talking to God. She took the communion bread and felt clean for the first time in years.

The transformation was miraculous. From a miserable, self-centred depressive, Maeve was suddenly telling the doctors and nurses, 'I'm cured, I really am. God has done it.' She could sense the reluctance to admit it in their answers; she realised they thought she had finally flipped and gone mad, but even that failed to annoy her.

It was the following day when Maeve was talking to another patient that she happened to look through the glass doors and see Marion. Somehow Marion had managed to find out where she was and decided to visit. As their eyes met Marion pushed open the door and they raced towards each other to swamp one another in hugs and kisses. Marion burst out, 'Have you accepted Jesus?' It was the only way she could have imagined such a transformation.

Maeve looked her in the eyes and replied: 'Yes, I do believe I have.'

Marion gave her friend a Bible, which became an instant companion. As they talked Marion told Maeve: 'It has to be the work of the Holy Spirit. It is unbelievable.'

It was. Eight days later Maeve was allowed to leave. Her first stop was her small flat where she flushed down the toilet the remnants of her drug collection. She worked for a while cooking for a Roman Catholic order of men in their community, and then joined the mission organisation Operation Mobilisation which she now works with in Brussels as a book-keeper and secretary. Life, for Maeve George, came at forty-one. And she knows it. With Jesus as a constant companion she hasn't been lonely since.

7

Johan: Hunt for adventure

The explosion shivered the ground, and caused the blond 20-year-old Dutchman and his swarthy Israeli Arab friend to flatten themselves on the ground. Fragments of earth spattered over their figures and the air was cut by the shrill squeal of a cow, a rear leg severed by the blast. The beast bellowed, and then groaned, the brown-and-white form convulsing, a memorial to the land-mines hastily strewn by Syrian forces six years before in the area bordering the River Jordan.

Johan Schep shook the debris from his long, blond hair and prodded his companion. 'Let's get the animal,' he muttered. Together they inched over the three or four yards of earth separating them from the wounded cow and dragged it through the rusting, rickety barbed-wire gate. A quick inspection of the cow's ear confirmed Johan's suspicions; his hand reached for a pair of scissors from the glove compartment on his jeep and proceeded to carefully snip the hair from a small patch on the brown, heaving flanks. His cutting revealed what he was looking for—an aged 'Z' brand, burned into the flesh by the Jewish owner years before.

He looked at Mohamed and grinned. Together they heaved the inanimate body into the back of the jeep, jumped into the front seats and scorched up the road towards the distant police station.

Johan swaggered inside and rapped on the desk. When the officer appeared he looked slightly bored. 'I thought I told you to go away,' he scowled. 'The cows belong to the old man, we told you. Now leave me in peace.'

Johan motioned the officer outside, pointing to the dying cow in the jeep. A slight flicker of interest crossed the policeman's brow and he followed the European into the searing heat of the Israeli sun. 'There,' said Johan, triumphantly pointing to the small area he had cleared, 'is our brand. Here are the documents to prove it.' He rifled in his pocket and brought out a sheaf of papers, handing them to the police officer. 'And that is a fresh cut—hardly a week old,' he added. The officer reached out and felt the cow's ear, fingering the V-shaped notch and admitting that the scar was still fresh.

'It seems that you are right,' he admitted. 'Take the animal and go.'

'We want the others,' Johan reminded him. 'There are another thirty of our animals in that field. You can check the brands as we bring them out if you wish.'

'Take what is yours,' replied the by-now bored official, adding with a smirk, 'You know that's a minefield they are grazing in, don't you?'

'We know, and we'll get them.'

Johan and Mohamed returned to the edge of the field and surveyed the thirty or so animals tugging the short, sparse growth from the earth. When an elderly man appeared, waving his arms and roaring that the cows were his, Johan nodded towards the police officer who had followed them. 'They have his brand,' the officer confirmed. The man slunk away to leave Johan and Mohamed waving straw and succeeding in attracting a couple of animals, which wandered noisily over to be grabbed and attached to a length of rope. Another cow followed, but the earth erupted under her and she crashed to the earth in a thunder of explosive force.

'I'm going to drive them out,' Johan called out, picking his way over a small loose-brick wall as he hurried alongside the field. He reached the weed-dressed banks of the river, pushing through the towering reeds until he faced the field. There was no fence this side—only the signs threatened death. He began to walk into the field.

A flash of light along a silvered, raised edge of metal reminded him that he was in a minefield. Carefully he picked his way along, following the footprints of cattle in the soft earth of the field, waving his arms and calling out as he did so. Gradually the cattle slunk towards the gate to be grabbed by a grateful Mohamed. Three more times the terrible noise of an explosion was to rock the afternoon before the couple stood with the remains of their herd, and five dying or wounded bodies.

While Johan ferried the bodies to the field from which they had begun the search more than a week before, Mohamed trekked along keeping the cattle moving, over the iron bridge which spanned the

River Jordan and back to Rosh Pinna. Johan
returned to help his friend, keeping the jeep slowly
moving behind the procession until they reached
the sanctuary of their own land. While Johan was
locking the gate behind the last of the cows
Mohamed was gesticulating and talking to his wife
and neighbours. Johan was suddenly swallowed up
in the plump darkness of Mohamed's mother, tears
in her eyes and the tone of her voice letting him
know that, despite his lack of Arabic, he must
never, never do such a foolish thing again as to walk
in a minefield: he looked into the watering eyes,
smiled sheepishly and nodded agreement.

It had been a hard week. In fact, he reckoned, it
had been a hard life . . .

The second son in a large family of eight children,
Johan began life on a farm in the little village of
Lexmond, alongside the river Lek near Utrecht,
Holland. It was a farming community in which his
father was a patriarchal figure—landowner, church
leader and on the village committee—and his
mother worked long hours but always seemed to
find time for the embroidery she loved, and to
spend time with her children and the many visitors
who popped into the farm.

Johan loved the farm. But he almost didn't live
long enough to appreciate it. When he was three he
spotted his father using one oar to manoeuvre the
flat-bottomed boat away from the small canal that
ringed the field alongside the house, and raced out
to watch. As he reached the edge of the canal Johan
slipped, scrabbled for a fraction of a second on the
muddy bank before plopping head first into the

muddy water, his wooden clogs drifting down-stream.

Somehow his mother had an instinct that forced her to rush from the house, spotting the little red trousers—all that was visible of her son—waggling above the water. She jumped into the mud and dragged him out with the help of neighbours and their flat-bottomed boat. For several minutes she pressed her young son's chest, pumping out the filthy water and mud and injecting life back into his lungs. Spluttering he came to, unaware that only an unknown instinct and the vigilance of his mother had kept him alive.

When Johan was five disaster did strike the household. Playing with his younger brother, Jan, just before they went to sleep, they grabbed apples, laid out to dry in their large room, and threw them at selected targets. When their father's angry face appeared, demanding to know who had thrown the apples, Johan shifted the blame on to his younger brother, who was told off. The following day Jan was killed in a car accident as he crossed the road. Standing alongside the small grave in the village churchyard, Johan sobbed as he recalled his dis-honesty and the fact that he was now unable to apologise. It was a memory that would haunt the youngster for many years.

Life was hard on the farm. As more brothers and sisters were born—the family eventually reached seven—it seemed that Mother's life was a constant round of having a baby and then growing fat on the next, and Johan almost booked an annual visit to the neighbouring farm to which he was sent, only to return after the birth of another brother or sister.

But he loved the farm and in particular the cows. In the morning he helped his father feed them and after school he raced home to be on hand to help at milking time—particularly his favourite, Ida, named after his mother. The sad-looking red cow seemed to sense the gentle touch of the little fellow as he sat on the three-legged wooden stool and eased the milk from her teats, to squirt it into the bucket with a metallic sound until the bucket began to fill. The little farmer's boy knew all the cows; their peculiarities, likes and dislikes. The smell of the cowshed, the open fields and the sight of the water flowing through the canals, pumped from the river by a windmill on the edge of the village, was an idyllic existence.

His father was determined to bring up his children well. Three times a day after meals he would use his brawny arms to clear a space in front of him on the dining table, reach into the cupboard alongside him and get the family Bible, a small, battered, black book. In a sombre voice Father would read a passage and then pray, pausing only to ensure that all the family had their eyes closed at the appropriate time.

The children also had to go to church—sitting in a neat line alongside Mother while Father, an elder, sat at the front eyeing them occasionally to make certain they were paying attention. It was all too much for the second son. What turned him off religion even more was that he was told that his school-friend, whose parents were not Christians, could not be a Christian because, unlike Johan, he hadn't been baptised. In his youthful mind Johan couldn't bring himself to care about a God who didn't love someone who couldn't help it if his parents refused to baptise him . . .

Before he was married, Johan's father had been in the army, nearly four years of his service being spent in Indonesia. As he saw farmers and friends emigrating to other parts of the world to begin new lives he began to hanker for foreign parts too. Brochures began to appear round the house extolling the virtues of South America. The advice of an uncle who had left for Brazil finally told, and the Scheps decided to leave Holland.

Johan, at eleven years of age, sensed the traumatic happenings as they occurred, the most upsetting being when he watched crowds of fellow farmers packing the family farmyard to bid for their possessions. He saw the small herd of cows paraded in front of the crowd one at a time and heard the auctioneer rattle off calculations rapidly before banging the gavel onto a makeshift desk erected in front of the house. And he watched as Ida was walked along the processional route, showing her features to the audience, and looked on in horror as his beloved pet was bought, pushed into a lorry and driven off.

A coach was booked to take the family and friends to the harbour in Antwerp ready for their new life. Johan looked out of the window as the windmills, polders and dykes passed by, the conversation of uncles, aunts and grandparents seeming inconsequential to his young mind.

Packed into a couple of cabins on board the enormous liner he began to enjoy life again and taste new adventures—marbles with his brothers on the rolling deck (occasionally losing some of the

precious spheres over the side of the ship); hide-
and-seek in the never-ending labyrinth of corridors
and steps; exciting new lands to explore when the
ship stopped; and slithering across the greasy pole
perched precariously over the ship's swimming pool
only to be pushed in and baptised by King Neptune
when they crossed the Equator.

Only the food was disagreeable: to the Dutch
family everything seemed to contain garlic, so they
existed on porridge and apple sauce, a diet adopted
by other Dutch families on the French ship.

Eventually they arrived at Rio de Janeiro, the
towering statue of Jesus Christ, arms outstretched,
being easily visible on the hillside overlooking the
city but hardly rating a glance from the children
more anxious to inspect the city. They did that in
file, trailing behind Father and the uncle who had
come to meet them, much to the amazement of a
traffic policeman who stopped the cars to allow the
crocodile of blond Dutch children across.

Coaches were waiting to take the newcomers to
the farms allotted to them and as they jolted along
the South American roads Johan stared at the
shanty homes and the brown-skinned inhabitants
in amazement.

Later, as his father saw the sunburnt noses of the
children on the colony, the red earth from which he
was to make a living, and the scant growth in the
fields, he turned to Mother in discouragement:
'Where have I brought my family? What have I
done?'

Mother slipped an arm round his back and spoke
soothingly. 'It's early days yet. We'll make out,
you'll see.' Always positive, Mother soon had him
on his feet again.

Water was a major problem—it had to be brought in huge tanks by tractor from a well four miles away. It meant that no longer was water the easy-to-use commodity it had been in Holland. Now it was rationed. The farmhouse was a shack with a wooden floor and three rooms—one for the children, five boys and two girls,—one for the parents, and a living-room-cum-kitchen. The children slept on mattresses on the floor. Light was provided at night by oil lamps.

For a month or so things began to slip into a new routine, until Johan began to have pains in his stomach. For a couple of days he struggled to school, the weekend break providing him with a short holiday with the family of a friend. The friend's farm had cows and he enjoyed milking them and rounding them up but within hours of arriving he was sent to bed clutching his stomach in agony. All weekend he lay on the bed until Father appeared on Sunday evening, still wearing the sombre suit he had worn to church. As soon as he saw Johan, Father picked up his son saying, 'I'll take you to hospital.' He had had appendicitis himself and knew the signs. Laying the boy in the back of the tractor he began the jolting drive to the hospital, twenty miles away. All the way the boy cried with pain, one sudden spasm bringing a scream to his lips until he eventually passed out.

When he came to it was in the hospital—an operation had shown his appendix had burst.

Ten days later he was allowed home, still in a great deal of pain. 'It will get better,' the doctor promised, but it didn't. For six months he slept in a bed made up in his parents' room so that they could watch over him; his wound didn't seem to want to heal, suppurating continually. It was there that he observed his father, every evening, kneeling by the side of his bed, his lips moving as if in conversation, but talking to no one. Johan couldn't understand who Father was talking to.

Another operation discovered that a swab of bandage had been left inside Johan from the previous surgery—when that was removed healing followed quickly, but the months of illness had left their mark in the shape of a bulging stomach. At school his friends began to call him 'Johan with the beer belly' and an inferiority complex developed.

Johan's father, however, decided to return to Holland. Life in Brazil had not been the adventure he had anticipated; but leaving was an expensive business, the family selling their belongings for only a fraction of the value. When they arrived back in Holland—the return journey was by air—it was to a very different existence to that of two years before when they had left. Father, the one-time landowner, farmer, key man in the village community, took the first job he could get—loading sacks of pig food on to a lorry to deliver them to the farmers he had once given directions to.

After a time the family moved to the town of Leerdam where Father became a farm worker on a large estate and they were given a house with the job. Things settled down with a regular wage, a home, and stability, but Johan, now thirteen and short of schooling because of his long sickness in Brazil, tried unsuccessfully to catch up in high school.

Two years later and they were once more on the move: Father bought the goodwill and round from a milkman in Gorinchem, a neatly fortified town dating back to the thirteenth century. As his father's milk round built up Johan tried for his third year at high school, the distance from home making transport a necessity. He bought a motor bike and rode alongside his elder brother, Kees. The ten-mile trip was fun on the motor cycles—if a little cold in the winter—but Johan added spice to the journey by coaxing extra speed out of the machine or taking diversions. One afternoon he rode towards a stationary vegetable lorry and decided to pass on the near side to give the driver a shock; it was Johan who got the shock when he discovered a telegraph pole in the way as he and the bike smashed into it at speed without a crash helmet. For six weeks he lay in a dark room, concussed, before regaining consciousness and putting on the same brave face he always tried to show.

The accident meant he had missed a vital examination so, faced with the option of another year at school, he decided to join his father, whose business had progressed as he delivered milk and groceries throughout the town. A keen talker and enthusiastic salesman, Johan began to extend the round and sell more. Eventually the three-wheeled wagon was swapped for the town's first large mobile shop, a big walk-around vehicle in which customers could buy a wide variety of groceries.

Business began to boom until a supermarket opened up in the town and the family couldn't compete with its cut-price bargains. Now the money spent on goodwill was wasted: customers disappeared overnight, tempted by cheaper goods. The family faced another major problem; pilfering.

Money was disappearing from the accounts without trace and with several workers it was difficult to spot the thief.

Johan longed for an escape but even national service was closed to him; he discovered the local authorities had classified him as the family bread-winner. There was no alternative but to be tied to the business, which was running downhill.

For four years Johan worked with his father, admiring his upright, moral approach to business and life—he cheated no one—while Johan's only way of escape was the hippie scene. It was the time of Woodstock, hippie-mania; he allowed his blond hair to grow despite his parents' complaints, and dreamed of travelling the world.

When he told his parents they cut short his arguments. 'You can't go. The family needs you,' sobbed Mother. Father stoically reminded him: 'Son, you are the family business. The customers love you. Things will work out all right.'

Johan began to extend his range of friends, getting wilder in his hunt for pleasure—girls, drinking and wild living became his norm in the evenings and at weekends. He would return home in the late hours of Sunday morning bleary-eyed after a night with girls and hippie friends, and an hour or so later would be seated in the family pew in church, looking smart, if bored, by all that was happening. To avoid the lengthy sermons he decided to go out with the small children and tell them Bible stories. His escape route worked well: the dramatic way in which he told his tales endeared him to the youngsters who loved the embellishments he added for effect. One day the wife of a church elder listened to him. As the meeting ended she said quietly: 'Johan will pray'. There was silence. At nineteen years of age Johan reflected on his activities of the previous night when he had been sleeping with a girl in one of his wilder moments. He couldn't pray. Instead he began to weep and walked from the church.

At twenty-one he was hospitalised for an operation on a stomach ulcer which turned out to be good fortune in disguise. Brother Arie took his role in the business and slipped into it as if he had been born to the job. Within weeks he had discovered the culprits who had been stealing and business began to build up again.

When Johan left hospital after eight weeks of serious sickness, he was able to concentrate on the sun, freedom and excitement he had promised himself in different parts of the world. Australia, Canada and South Africa were considered but he finally opted for Israel. A Jewish customer on his milk round had talked about the country and the opportunities for youngsters on the kibbutzim.

So in September 1973 he left Schipol airport in Holland to the fond but sad farewells of his family, his belongings packed inside a deep-blue rucksack and with no ideas about his future. It was a flight of fancy—an endeavour to flee from his past and establish a new, exciting future. Johan had no idea of what he would do; that came when he found himself seated alongside a couple of other young Dutchmen on the four-hour flight. They too were looking for something different and were going to work on a kibbutz. But they had the address of an office in Tel Aviv where such work was distributed.

The trio shouldered their rucksacks and made straight for the office on landing, to be directed to a small kibbutz, Ammiad, north of the Sea of Galilee. A concrete bunker and the barbed-wire surround and occasional trench were reminders of the birth of the kibbutz less than thirty years ago when a group of Palmah trainees—the Israeli independence fighters—founded it and used it as their base during the 1948 battle that led to the birth of their nation.

Johan was put in a small hut, shared with another of his new Dutch friends, Ron. He rode a horse as he looked after the cattle roaming the fields adjacent to the kibbutz, but occasionally found himself in a less likeable craft—the box-like structure on the end of a small mobile crane which lifted him to the top of fruit trees for the apple-picking he didn't really enjoy. As a youngster born and brought up on a cattle farm he preferred the smell of the hay and the snuffling of the cows, to the backache which followed fruit picking.

For three weeks the trio worked happily, until the Jewish holiday, Yom Kippur, emptied the kibbutz. Several of the two hundred and fifty or so kibbutzniks were religious and went to the synagogue, while others enjoyed themselves. The three Dutch men spent the morning in the nearby rocky hills, investigating caves, drinking cans of beer and revelling in the freedom and sunshine. Their return to the kibbutz, however, ended the day of relaxation. It was Yom Kippur, the Day of Atonement, 6 October, 1973: in a surprise attack Egyptian forces had crossed the Suez Canal in force and at the same time the Syrians had invaded the Golan Heights they had lost in the bitter Six-Day War of six years ago.

On the kibbutz all the young Israeli men were putting on the uniforms which were always in readiness and checking their rifles before making for emergency call-up points.

Only the young women with babies were left— the unmarried women had left for the front line along with the men. Johan helped them into the concrete air-raid shelter during the evening, and pitched in looking after babies, changing nappies and feeding those children that drank from bottles as well as those who ate solid food.

A bomb exploded nearby, the shelter reverberating with the massive shock waves; and gunfire could be heard in the distance. The Syrians, he thought, must be getting closer.

Next day a message came through from a mosjav (co-operative village) towards the Golan Heights: a herd of cows had escaped and wandered all over the area—but the men were all in the army. They needed help. Johan, keen to find every vestige of excitement he could, volunteered. Later that day a doctor called and, as he was driving to the mosjav, Johan hitched a lift. Along the route they passed tanks and army vehicles trundling towards the front line; gun emplacements dotted the roadside and women were handing food and drink to soldiers. Overhead Johan watched aeroplanes cartwheeling in combat; he saw one burst into flame and scream like an injured animal until it crashed into the distant pink and blue mountains; another whined low overhead, a smudge of smoke trailing behind.

The adventure he craved was coming in full. Up ahead the Israeli army was fighting a desperate battle to hold its positions. Johan arrived at Mosjav

Almagor, the settlement, and was immediately given a yellow jeep for the search and introduced to Mohamed, an Israeli Arab who would help. The jeep was packed with barbed wire, nails and tools and the pair, with other Arab help, began mending fences and catching those cattle that were within a short distance of the now-secure fields. As passing Israeli soldiers began to speak with more confidence of the war—despite appalling losses—Johan too began to have success. Most of the three hundred cattle had been discovered and herded into the safety of the fenced-off ranges when they set off to hunt the final thirty or so.

It became apparent that the erring cattle had probably wandered across the River Jordan, low at the time, so Johan and Mohamed drove over the bridge to extend their search. It was then that Mohamed spotted the cattle, and the minefield rescue took place.

Back in Mosjav Almagor Johan was hailed as a celebrity: when the farmer returned from the war he gave the Dutchman a signed statement of his ability as a herdsman—and three prime beef cattle as a gift. For four months Johan enjoyed life with the Arabs, sharing their food and sitting round the fire at night with the men, trying to capture the language as they talked.

As peace returned Johan decided to move on. A few days previously he had met a Canadian who was returning home to get married, but without time to sell a car that was identified on his visa. Johan agreed to sell the vehicle for him, had his visa marked with the necessary identification, and promised to send on the money. The once cream-

coloured Volkswagon coupé didn't rate a buyer in
Haifa, so Johan decided to use the vehicle as his
transport down south to the resort of Eilat where
prospects were better. The long journey was broken
only by a stream of hitch-hikers; a gesture which
was to cost him heavily as the vehicle's engine
spluttered to a halt in Eilat with garage attention
high on its list of requirements.

Johan wasn't worried. The beautiful, warm, clear
air of Israel's premier winter resort, the soft murmur of the Red Sea, and the distant hills of Jordan
across the water were just the sights he had longed
for. A nearby hippie encampment welcomed him
and within hours he had created his own home, a
patchwork building of corrugated iron, wooden
boxes, boards and palm leaves.

On New Year's Eve he sat on the beach, trickling
the fine silver sand through his fingers, and looking
at the stars, glittering in the clearest sky he had ever
observed. He found himself singing a song from his
childhood, 'Whatever my future may bring, the
Lord's hand will guide me.' 'There must be a God;
there must be a maker,' he pondered as he studied
the heavens. 'But how,' he wondered, 'can I ever
know him?'

Despite his beautiful surroundings, Johan was
puzzled by a religion which didn't seem to mean
much.

New Year's Day. A bleaching sun began to give
extra heat to the rickety walls of Johan's makeshift
cabin in the wadi outside Eilat. He woke up,
rubbed his eyes and lifted his body from the floor. A
breakfast of bananas and coffee, boiled over a hast-
ily-lit fire in the small stove he had fashioned out of

bricks and cement taken from a nearby building site, fortified him. He left the hut and wandered down to the beach, his eyes flickering across the bodies already positioned for sunbathing, looking for fresh faces. A quick swim in the crystal-clear waters of the Red Sea and Johan returned to the beach, relaxing in the shade of a palm tree, his back resting easily against the oddly-shaped trunk. As he sat he saw ships bobbing on the water and occasionally a larger vessel smoothly ploughing its way towards the distant port of Aqaba on the Jordanian side of the gulf. Johan began to dream of the places the ships had visited and would travel to . . .

A voice interrupted his thoughts.

'I have been a sailor and it isn't as exciting as you think.' A tall, blond-haired man with a straggling beard bent over him, speaking in a Dutch accent.

'I was just imagining what it would be like to go on a long journey to distant lands,' Johan said.

'It's no different from sitting here. I have sailed round the world and my troubles went with me. Wherever you go there is no way out of the circle of life. I have seen other countries and discovered that people all over the world have the same needs and ask the same questions.'

The man moved on, leaving Johan puzzled at the briefness of the encounter. He saw the Dutchman speak to a group of people nearby and listened.

'You need to be born again,' he heard. 'Not in the flesh like this,' went on the stranger stretching out his arm and pinching the flesh to demonstrate, 'but spiritually. God wants to give you a new life. It happened to me just a few weeks ago. I read in the Bible that Jesus said, "Come to me, all you who are tired from carrying heavy loads, and I will give you rest," and I discovered it was true. Jesus gave me that rest. Now I am free and happy . . .'

Johan could see from his eyes that he believed and meant what he was saying. For him God was real.

Johan went back to his makeshift hut considering the words he had heard. The relaxed style of living in the hippie community suited him: his freedom and the sheer bliss of having sun, sand and sea were all he wanted and gradually the message he had overheard dribbled from his mind. He enjoyed the friendship of the other hippies, sitting for hours talking, sometimes smoking hashish cigarettes, and then sleeping with girls. He began to study his world map to plot the next country he would visit. There was, however, a major problem before he could leave: he still had the car marked on his visa and a so-called friend, who had taken it into his garage to mend, seemed reluctant to do so. Johan pressed and was merely promised a future date.

He began to get angry, which turned to a deeper dependence on drugs and drink.

One evening as he rummaged through his rucksack for the tin in which he kept his cigarettes he felt something hard—it rustled; out of the interior came the small Bible his mother had insisted he took with him on his journey when he had first left Holland. Idly he flicked through the pages and began to read. 'Freedom is what we have—Christ has set us free! Stand, then, as free people, and do not allow yourselves to become slaves again.' The words from Galatians 5:1 speared his heart. Was this the key to his search—that freedom was in

Jesus Christ ? Not in a church, or a religion, or a set
of rules, but in a person ? He began to read in
earnest, beginning with the Gospels and imagining
the figure of Jesus performing the many incredible
feats achieved during his lifetime. 'He was the super
hippie,' thought Johan. Then he read of Jesus'
death and realised that it was not simply so that
Jesus could atone for the sins of the world, but
especially for him—Johan Schep! Jesus, the one
with a perfect life, had gone to the Cross for him.

Shame filled Johan as he thought of the way he
was living, the drugs, drink and girls . . . Gradually, so gradually, light began to filter into his dark
mind; just as the waves of the sea were impercept-
ible but were suddenly lapping the shore, Johan
discovered he was overcoming more of the influ-
ences of his past and trying harder to be a Christian. He had always considered Christianity
perfectly in order for others but not for him: 'I was
afraid to claim it because of my background,' he
said when he met the Dutchman, John, again.
Slowly and surely Jesus became the person that
Johan loved, but it was a major battle.

He became a regular attender at Bible studies in
a flat in Eilat and began to realise just what the
battle entailed: it was to be an all-out victory for
Jesus, or life wasn't worth living.

Relaxing on the beach one day, Johan watched a
group of friends make their way down to the water's
edge. As he looked at them, laden down with their
rucksacks, it was as if God was speaking to him,
pointing out that he too had been carrying an enormous weight on his back—the weight of sin from
the past which was getting heavier by the day.

Johan imagined Jesus had loosened the weight and sent it spinning away never to be seen again—just the realisation of that helped Johan feel cleaner and sense peace, and the continued new life kept stirring within him. He began to talk to other hippies and holidaymakers about Jesus, taking them to John when his own meagre knowledge fell short.

Finally he managed to get back the car and take it to the customs office to have it struck from his record. 'I never again want to be trapped by material things,' he told God as he prayed that evening.

When John met a beautiful Jewish girl who was starting to believe in Jesus Johan saw instantly—before John did—that the couple were made for each other; Johan began to make plans to leave Israel. As he left them for the airport John stuffed a huge wedge of Christian leaflets into Johan's rucksack. At Ben Gurion he got off the bus and turned to the first man he could see, anxious to demonstrate to himself that he could witness without John. As he took a leaflet from his bag and tapped the man on the arm the man swung round, punched him on the nose and stormed off. Johan yanked the heap of leaflets from his bag and dumped them in the nearest waste-paper bin. That, he decided, was the end of witnessing to his faith!

He made for Greece and from Athens went to the port of Piraeus and took a boat to the island of Ios where life took a downward surge. He lived in a donkey's hut with a girl; swimming naked, sleeping together, taking drugs and working at nights in a discotheque serving drinks and playing records, trying to forget God. It was the craziest period of his life. Deeper and deeper he sank—completely wild and uninhibited. The Bible stayed in his rucksack and he felt guilty just knowing it was there.

He returned home in April for his parents' twenty-fifth wedding anniversary and they welcomed him. His old girlfriend also made him welcome—too welcome in fact, as one evening he was tempted to have sex on the beach and she then told him she was pregnant. The news stunned him into agreeing to announce their engagement. But when his parents presented him with an ironing board as a gift it brought the reality of marriage to him: this wasn't what Johan intended to get out of life at all. He didn't want to be cooped up in a house, he preferred the lure of unknown places. The shock went to his brain and he had a nervous breakdown, losing his job as a truck driver after smashing the vehicle twice in eight days.

The doctor prescribed a series of tablets and the minister warned Johan, 'Don't do things like this to your parents. They don't deserve it after all they have done for you.'

As Johan puzzled over his future with his mind still racing John walked into the house. He had broken a journey to America where he was to marry his Jewish girlfriend, Judy. He stood by Johan, sensed the deep turmoil in his friend's mind, and advised him to throw away the engagement ring. 'It's no way to start married life,' he warned.

When his friend had gone Johan hadn't the courage to take his advice but he was reminded, simply by John's presence, of the time he had felt free: when he had tried to follow Jesus Christ. Kneeling by his bed that evening as he had watched his father do during the months of his illness in Brazil, Johan prayed. He called on God to release him from the oppression that was tying his mind in knots and to fill him with peace. It was as if a red curtain came down on him—a curtain created by the blood of Jesus Christ. As it covered him he felt the oppression leave. He felt forgiven. His mind was at rest and peace flooded into his heart. If trying to live the Christian life had been difficult before, now he felt confident that Jesus was in him, taking over every area of his life.

It was as if the wheels of his life had finally lifted from the tarmac of his old life and he was steadily getting higher in a new existence with his maker.

He had been so shocked at the results of sin—the pleasure that only brought death and destruction—that he began to seek God with all his heart, determined to share with others the good news that Jesus can live inside a life, changing it and recreating it.

Just as he came to terms with being engaged, his wife-to-be announced that she wasn't pregnant after all. With the threat of an enforced marriage no longer over him Johan called off the engagement.

At twenty-three with a new future ahead of him he wanted to be an agricultural missionary, but his lack of schooling and a dead-end job on a farm made him realise that wouldn't work. Then he became leader on a children's farm where youngsters from deprived backgrounds learnt about animals, had fun and spent their holidays in the farming environment. It was enjoyable—and he was paid for it. Johan decided it was what God wanted him to do. When the farm closed to visitors in the winter he simply went back to Eilat to help

John and Judy in the different areas of witness they were involved in. They had been married in America and returned to Israel as new immigrants. Because they had little money Johan returned to Mosjav Almagor in Galilee and sold the three cows he had been given, using the money to buy a washing machine for Judy and spending the remainder on Bibles to give away. Johan pitched his tent in the desert and discovered it was constantly full of young people and travellers wanting to know about his faith.

The Dutchman became Johan the Jesus boy, the traveller with the Bible. When he needed money he simply went to work for a short time in the melon fields or helping John in an experimental farm. For two years he enjoyed the dual existence: the summer camp with the children in Holland and winter in the desert. All the time he loved talking about Jesus and how through repentance Jesus changed lives. When the camp job ended he worked full-time in the desert for five years until 26 April 1982, when the Sinai was given back to Egypt and he was forced to move away from the oasis across the new border. He merely decided to witness anywhere in the country, spending time in a hospital in Haifa when the war with Lebanon reached a peak, helping Israeli soldiers, Syrians, Lebanese and children—trying to bring healing and at the same time praying for their inner peace.

Accepting an invitation to work at Capernwray Bible School, near the English Lake District, having studied there for a few months to improve his Bible knowledge, Johan became a helper to the students, looking after their personal lives and encouraging them in practical witnessing. And in the summer he was free not only to go back to the desert, but to take young volunteers from the college to witness alongside him.

Even a serious back operation didn't deter him from talking about Christ. Sent to see a specialist in London, when the series of consultations was over, Johan presented the doctor with a plant, a Bible and his testimony. A few days later he learned that he was the last patient to see that doctor, who died of a heart attack an hour after the consultation. Johan realised that the brevity of life meant he must tell everyone he could about his new life in Jesus Christ.

The minefield he had foolishly walked through in Galilee had been merely a picture of his previous passage through life; damage and destruction on all sides. Now, however, he had a guide, Jesus Christ. As he told his parents: 'I can walk safely because Jesus is alongside me. He not only lives in my heart, but he watches over my life every step I take.

'He will lead me and I now live with the greatest assurance that life can give—simply that one day I will be with my Lord Jesus for all eternity.'

8

Ahmad: In a strange land

Nestling in the palm of Ahmad's hand the small, black, plastic-covered book carried the promise of a new future: a life full of excitement. It was his passport to adventure. The very name on the cover brought a thrill to him: *Seefahrtsbuch*—his seaman's journal.

Staring back at him from the first page was the grim-faced black-and-white photograph of himself, Ahmad Turkamani, a 20-year-old trainee mariner; a man desperate to escape the past. The log-book was slipped into his pocket alongside the green-covered Lebanese passport. Together they were his tickets to paradise and riches.

Ahmad peered from the bleak window of his room in the seamen's school in Bremervörde, West Germany, at the grey sky and scudding rain, and dreamed of the cloudless, sun-drenched home he had left in Lebanon.

Ahmad was born in the small town of Halba in the north of Lebanon, a few miles north of Tripoli and a short journey from the country's northern border with Syria. His first three years were spent in the home of his grandparents, the whole family slept crammed into one small room—his parents, grandparents, himself and, for the final twelve months, his younger brother. Another room housed the animals, a couple of cows and a camel, with their foodstuff stacked in a small storage area on one side. A little kitchen completed the dwelling—all three rooms fanning out from a small open-air courtyard in which his father, grandfather and other men from the town would talk in the evenings round a fire drinking hot, sweet tea. At the rear of the house were terraces packed with olive, apricot and fig trees and grape vines while the ground beneath them was cultivated to grow vegetables.

Ahmad's father was keen to progress in the world and refused to contemplate his eldest son and heir becoming a poor farmer like his own father. Instead Ahmad was groomed for the best that could be offered to him. Just as his grandmother had sold pots and pans, and worked in the fields alongside her husband to earn money to send her son to school, and then to high school for further education, so Ahmad was being encouraged to be studious, to take advantage of every educational opportunity life offered.

When he was three his father bought another plot of land and, despite the protestations of Grandfather, built a four-roomed house on it and moved his family. The home included a garage and Ahmad's father, a financial official in the local government offices in Tripoli, was soon driving one of the rare cars in the town—an olive-green two-door

Vauxhall. If Grandfather, with his beard and Arab head-dress, was one of the town's elder statesmen, Father was among the up-and-coming young leaders, determined to get on in life and ensure that his family followed his pattern.

But Ahmad preferred standing alongside Grandfather, digging in the fields, to school work. He would rather watch Grandfather unroll his rush prayer mat and kneel to Allah than spend time in study. Ahmad was beginning to develop two urges that would be conflicting emotions within him for many years: a hunger for religious peace of mind, and a craving for excitement.

The religion was partly introduced by Grandfather, who prayed five times a day, hardly missed a visit to the local mosque, and would spend hours with Ahmad sitting at his knee listening in rapt attention to the stories of the adventures of Mohamed, or other tales from the Koran.

Ahmad began to sample adventure early in life. In his young teens he and a friend locked themselves in his room, shut the windows tightly, and sucked away at cigarettes packed with hashish. As his mind swam in a hundred directions at once it seemed the ultimate experience.

A more legitimate experience was when he was selected to represent his school in the national shot-putt event in the schools athletics championships in Beirut. His first visit to the nation's capital city, in the mini-bus driven by a teacher, was made complete when he kicked his leg, stretched his arm and flung the shot far enough to grab third place and a bronze medal. His appearance at home and in school the following day was like a hero's reception. The pleasure lasted for days.

When he was twelve he was still looking for something different, something less arduous than the boring lessons at school in which he was rarely able to shine. With a friend he went out shooting birds, taking instead of his own almost new rifle an ancient long-barrelled rifle from the corner where it rested in his grandfather's home. The delicately fashioned brass-work on the handle, and the smooth barrel, had always attracted the young would-be marksman. Unfortunately the birds didn't oblige the two sharp-shooters until late in the afternoon when a flock began to circle at the far end of the field—too far away for a successful shot.

When the friend got bored and returned Ahmad called after him: 'I'm going to shoot something.' He raised the weighty gun, tracking the flight of a gaggle of birds. His left hand held the barrel tightly as he peered through the worn sights and squeezed the trigger. The crack of the percussion cap in the shell was met with a simultaneous explosion as the gun-barrel shattered, blasting the tips off two of Ahmad's fingers. He grabbed a handkerchief and wrapped it round the bloodied stumps, running as he did so towards his home clutching the damaged rifle.

The church in the town seemed to rock, and then circle round in Ahmad's bleary vision, as he stumbled to the door of his house, to be rushed to hospital in Tripoli by relatives. Later in the day his father shuffled into the ward to gaze at his son in bed. Ahmad smiled up at him.

'Is it really only your fingers that were injured, son?' Father asked, leaning down to run his hands over the body of his eldest child, tears shining on his cheeks.

'Yes, Father—only my fingers. I'm all right, really I am.'

Being the eldest son had given Ahmad a position of respect and responsibility in the family.

In the town Ahmad's father was something of a celebrity. Named Omar—the Long-living One—because apart from himself and one sister, none of the other fourteen children born to his parents had lived through childhood. He was determined that his son should have all the advantages in life that he had been unable to take. Despite knowing that his son was obviously not destined for the life of a lawyer or doctor—the school reports made that clear—Omar was still desperately angry when 16-year-old Ahmad and his younger brother disappeared to join a squad of Palestinian recruits training for guerilla incursions into neighbouring Israel.

Like many youngsters they were bitterly disappointed with the Arabs' defeat at the hands of Israel in the Six Day War, and the rising tide of nationalism bore them along with it. Ahmad and Mohamed, two years his junior, had signed on in Beirut, been given forged documents in false names and taken through Syria to Jordan to begin desert training with experienced liberation fighters. Their intention was clear-cut: learn how to fight and then join raiding parties across the border into the Western Occupied Zone, killing Israeli soldiers. Even the possibility that they might die did not deter them.

But the arrival of their father at the camp in Jordan quashed those hopes. Somehow he had learned of their whereabouts and followed, demanding to speak with them in front of the camp commander. The two youths were taken before the commander to be lectured by their father.

'Come home, sons, this is no life for you,' he pleaded.

'But we want to kill Israelis. Our leaders have let us down badly, losing the Six Day War, and we want to pay the Israelis back for what they did to our countries. We want to fight,' the brothers insisted.

'Your mother is always crying, she is not well and wants you to come home. Come home for a time to cheer her up—then return to fight later,' Father cried.

Before the boys could answer the commander made up their minds, ordering them to return home . . .

Within weeks they had learned of a raid into the Galilee area in which many of their friends had been killed. The brothers did not return to the desert camp.

Ahmad's growing dissatisfaction with life in the Lebanese town provided the fertile ground for a suggestion from a close friend to take root. Mohsen had decided to become a sailor and was all set to go to Tripoli to a special training school where he could gain some preliminary knowledge before travelling to Western Germany for real training. Ahmad joined Mohsen in Tripoli at a sailing institute. Medicine and the law were closed to him, his school results had guaranteed that, but the sea promised a completely new life—a life of adventure and excitement. Within a few months he had mastered the basics and was ready to join Mohsen who had earlier travelled to Germany.

Omar didn't mind his son going to Germany; by then he had recognised that his eldest boy was not going to follow the direction he had planned for him, and considered that at least the life of a sea captain was respectable and a worthwhile profession. Delays in getting a visa meant it was not until 10 January that Ahmad took his suitcase and a small bag and boarded the Middle East Airline plane for Hamburg. Excitement gripped him as the mighty engines thundered to a full crescendo and plunged the craft the length of the runway and into the air. For the first time in his life Ahmad was flying—and for the first time too he felt that he was going to achieve something for the family and for his own personal pride.

Mohsen met his friend at the airport in Hamburg, taking him to the apartment in which he was staying for the evening. On the way the strange language fascinated Ahmad; would he master it? Early the next morning Mohsen accompanied him on the forty-minute train journey to Bremervörde and to the two-storey training school that was to be his home for the next ten weeks. Ahmad was placed in a room with an African and a German, neither of whom spoke Arabic. Already nearly two weeks behind on the lectures because of his delayed visa, he discovered it was hard going catching up on the lost ground in a language he had never spoken before. Fortunately the new intake included a number of Arabs, so he was able to try and copy their notes, but it was exceptionally difficult. The Arabs would get together often, trying to piece together the lectures—how to tie a multitude of different knots; basic navigation; the art of painting a ship; emergency procedures; and how to deal with fire on board.

Occasionally the students would be taken to a river and given practical training in a small twelve-seater rowing boat, taking it in turns to steer and direct the oarsmen in the bitingly cold European winter. It was all so very different from the warm, sunny climate Ahmad had left. And the early morning start—they began at 5.30 a.m.—was so different from life at home where mother did all the housework and prepared the food and he simply had to get out of bed and eat. But the worst privation of all was the food—especially pork which Ahmad and most of his Arab friends refused to eat. 'It is against our religious laws,' they protested, but there was never any substitute except for extra helpings of bread. It meant that Ahmad had to dip into the money his father had given him before he had left home, to supplement the diet, buying chicken in nearby restaurants. Even so, what to Ahmad had seemed an enormous amount of money when he left Lebanon was soon swallowed up by the higher prices of the Continent.

He was, however, passing the various tests during the course and beginning to understand what was expected of him.

Early on he was called into the principal's office and presented with a small black plastic-covered booklet. 'That is your seaman's log; in it will be recorded everything you do at sea, all the courses you take and all the ships you sail in. Look after it well,' he was told. It was that book which promised so much. And when he saw the principal stamp the first page and sign it to indicate that he had passed his initial training, Ahmad knew that the world was his oyster: now he would show his family what he could become; he was on the first rung to becoming a captain.

At the end of the course he was taken to the offices of a German shipping company and introduced to the manager. He was registered and given a short talk on the company and the ships under its flag. For Ahmad it was a strange feeling: he had still not mastered enough German to feel fluent and struggled to understand the people he met. But he did feel elated: he knew that school was now finished—he would only face a short course each year to continue his training until becoming a ship's captain.

The offices were in a house near Hamburg docks. Spartan, but neat, they were obviously used to interviewing foreigners who spoke hardly any German. Once he had signed the papers and become a staff sailor he was directed to a small hotel in Hamburg and told to wait until he was contacted. 'We shall find you a ship, so do nothing until we call you. When we call you will be given a job on board your first ship—then it is up to you,' he was told.

With better food, a room on his own, and a family running the hotel who treated him like a guest and made a fuss of him, Ahmad was ready to face the future.

The money he had brought with him from the Lebanon had almost gone, so Ahmad was very sparing with his cash. Fortunately the shipping company paid for the hotel but he received no money himself until he boarded his first ship, so it was a relief when eventually the phone call came: 'Be ready in the morning and I will collect you for your first ship.' He could understand no more of the message—but that was sufficient to guarantee the lonely Lebanese man a sleepless night, as he tossed and turned wondering what the following day would bring.

It brought the manager of the office to the hotel, driving a large luxurious Mercedes. Ahmad leaned into the leather upholstery and was taken to the docks with his suitcase. The manager hustled up the gangplank, motioning Ahmad to follow. Tentatively he did so, noticing at the same time the name *Elke Frese* on the side of the small 499BRT vessel. On board he was introduced to the first officer, smart and businesslike in his peaked cap and dark uniform. The gold buttons glinted and made Ahmad wish for the day when he too would wear such a uniform.

He was shown to a small cabin with two bunks, a small table and a wardrobe in which to pack his clothing, and while he was still claiming the bottom bunk and peering from the small port-hole at the end of the room, he heard a change in the sound of the engine and realised that the boat was on the move. His first journey as a sailor had begun.

Within minutes another crew member had introduced himself and invited Ahmad to eat with them before starting work. Sitting in the small dining area with the gabble of language going on all round, Ahmad realised he would need to learn German quickly if he wasn't going to be a lonely man. Within minutes of the meal finishing he had been appointed his first task: cleaning down part of the superstructure on the deck ready for painting. It was hard, unimportant work, but he buckled down to it, sensing that it was all part of the initial preparation he would have to undergo.

Later the first officer took him to his next job: 'Turkamani, I want you to clean the toilets.' Ahmad was aghast—this was women's work! He had never done manual work in his life before but he could put up with that—but cleaning toilets, no good Muslim would think of it. The orders were clear, however. Worse was to come: the first officer called out: 'I'll show you how; if you're a little shy, then you can do it on your own.' He grabbed a cloth and thrust his hand inside the pan, wiping the inside. 'Now do it!' he ordered, dropping the dripping cloth and walking off. Ahmad realised that being a sailor involved more than he had bargained with; but he did the job.

The sheer monotony of the work began to bore him: painting endlessly, washing the deck, scrubbing out the toilets—and always under grey European skies full of dark clouds, driving rain or even drifting snow. Worst of all, he was seasick. Lying in agony on his bunk he listened as his fellow sailors told him: 'Ahmad, you'll be worse if you keep lying here. Come up and work—it will take your mind off it.' He couldn't eat, and discouragement and disappointment filled his heart.

The journey lasted a month and twenty-two days—it seemed ten times longer—before the boat tied up again at Hamburg. 'I don't understand it,' Ahmad moaned to a fellow sailor as he tramped back to the hotel. 'We left loaded with coal, and at every port we stopped, we unloaded coal and loaded on more. And we've come back full of coal—why did we bother?' He began to hate coal as a cargo more than anything else; the dust filtered into every part of the ship, even his cabin. Every time they had to unload, helping to shovel or standing by guiding the huge jaws of the cranes into the hold to take gigantic mouthfuls of the black granules and spit it out into rail trucks, his clothes seemed to attract the minute particles and his face took on the appearance of a miner.

Two boats later Ahmad was beginning to dislike the sea as much as school—the constantly moving about, the language problem he couldn't conquer, and the attitudes of the sailors, which were against all he had ever been taught. 'They have no respect for each other—drinking and taking drugs—and stealing . . .' he told the motherly woman in the hotel in a moment of confession during one of his leave periods. 'I don't understand them at all.' But he was one of them and gradually began to adopt some of their bad habits.

The sailors knew where to buy drugs from; they were quick also to take up their full ration of duty-free tobacco, cigarettes and spirits ready to barter with it when they arrived at a new port. If that wasn't enough they had a black-market trade in part of the ship's cargo. No goods were safe from the lightning hands of the crew; they would steal and sell anything, pocketing the money, while all the while the captain looked the other way.

There was little to commend the life to Ahmad. He enjoyed the sun and freedom of foreign ports such as Honduras and the Dominican Republic, which he visited on his third ship. He met Arabic-speaking people for the first time in months and was able to spend two or three days in each city, making friends quickly with Arabs and visiting their homes.

If he thought that a new vessel would bring a change in fortunes, however, he was wrong: the next ship, *Baltic Concord*, brought discord and European weather once more. His disagreements with his fellow crew-members began to get more violent as despair ripped through him.

The taunts which sailors threw at each other without caring earned a violent reply from Ahmad. Only the drugs, bartering and women made his life bearable. In every port Ahmad would spend his hard-earned money on women, buying drinks and sexual favours all over the world as the list of ships he sailed on grew longer—America, Africa, Argentina, Yugoslavia, Spain, France, South Africa, Iraq, Philippines, Singapore; the countries and ports began to string out like well-worn worry-beads but he was still unhappy.

Most sailors settled on board a ship and stayed with it, but Ahmad's journal was rapidly becoming full of new entries. Each ship had its name stamped in and the dates of the voyages and service entered; Ahmad's had clocked up twelve entries when, on the 10,000-ton *Adolf Vinnen* in October 1973, he met one of the strangest crew-members he had travelled with—a Christian, Fritz Böme. The sailor was instantly named Jesus, or Christ, by the crew who grabbed every chance to tease and annoy him. Ahmad, by now weary of trying to impress others and much more likely to impress with his fists than with his capacity to reason, asked, 'Why do they persecute you ? You are a German like them? I can understand why they despise me—but not you.'

Fritz began to weep, sobbing, burying his head in his hands. 'They are angry because I am a Christian—I am trying to live like a Christian but it is very hard. It is almost too difficult for me.'

Fritz had been a Christian just a few months and began to talk with Ahmad in the privacy of his cabin. It was a revelation to the Muslim. 'But I thought every European was a Christian,' he said.

'No,' replied Fritz. 'Only people who have asked Jesus into their lives and live for him are Christians. I met some friends who told me all about what Jesus had done for me and I asked Jesus into my life. He has forgiven my sins and given me a new life—even though it is so hard.'

It was the loneliness of Fritz that impressed Ahmad more than what he said. Ahmad too had a lonely life—his fists had guaranteed him a single cabin and few friends. Now he discovered a sailor who didn't want to ridicule him.

He watched one day as Fritz read his Bible. 'Why do you read that book?' shouted a burly sailor. 'Put it away and read this,' he called out, flinging a pornographic magazine across the table.

Fritz went red, and left the room for his cabin, the food untouched. 'We have Jesus on board,' laughed the ribald sailor, drawing cheers from the remainder of the crew.

Ahmad went to comfort his new-found friend. He had already decided this would be his last voyage. The constant harassment had finally encouraged him to quit. Even the disgrace of going back to the Lebanon and his home village without any accomplishments was better than this life of stealing, womanising, and loneliness.

Fritz gave him books about Christianity, but they were difficult for the Muslim to read, couched as they were in high-level German and incorporating strings of difficult religious phrases he had never come across before. In any case he had little interest in being 'born again', one of the phrases he had heard Fritz use on many occasions.

As the boat docked, this time in Bremen, Ahmad made his way to a small hotel where he could think about his future and wait for the money due to him for his last voyage. The shipping company were slow to pay up. Every time he questioned them the promise was always 'come back next week—we are having problems sorting this out.' And his meagre savings were disappearing.

Entertainment was out of the reach of his wallet, so when Fritz invited him to meet a group of Christians for an evening Ahmad was ready; it was free and there might be food. They made their way along the Seilwall, a street leading away from the Weser canal in the city quite a way from the major dock area with which Ahmad had become familiar over the years.

Stopping at one of the houses, Fritz rang the bell and waited until a young man opened the door, smiled and invited them in. A meeting was in progress, so the two crept quietly into the centre of a group, sat on wooden chairs and listened. The bright, cheerful singing soon gave way to a young man who was obviously preaching but Ahmad could not catch all of the words—looking round the room, he realised he was probably the only foreigner.

As the service ended and he was being served with coffee and biscuits the young people began to chat with him as freely as his grasp of German would allow. It was all so strange: they were friendly and he enjoyed talking, for the first time realising that this group were interested in him and, unlike his sea-going companions, were not constantly throwing out nasty comments and cutting remarks. As they spoke about Christianity he described Islam and the Arab people—someone, he decided, ought to defend his own religion and race.

In the days that followed, as he vainly tried to get his money from the company, he spent a couple more evenings with the young Christian group. In the past Ahmad had always felt that the Germans he had met looked down on him, considering him primitive because he hadn't mastered their language, but here were people who didn't mind, who just wanted to be his friends. It was a unique feeling.

Then Fritz telephoned him at the hotel one day to report, 'I know you are running out of money and your company hasn't paid you your back pay yet, but I have spoken to the leader of the Christian group and he has agreed that you can live in the mission house free, if you wish.' Ahmad was overjoyed. He hardly needed to finger the few marks remaining in his pocket book before saying 'yes'. Within hours he was reporting to the mission with his luggage and being shown to one of the small bedrooms which he would share with a German, Wolfgang. It was too good to be true.

Wolfgang, who had quit the French Foreign Legion because of depression and then had become a Christian in Bremen when he had first met the group, proved a ready conversationalist, and the two spent hours each evening chatting about religion, each time with Ahmad beginning to realise a little more that there was something in Christianity he had not been aware of. On one occasion Wolfgang talked so much he suddenly realised it was morning, and had to leave for work without any sleep.

The feeling was even more difficult for Ahmad to comprehend a few days later, when he was woken early in the morning and, despite his complaints, ushered into the dining room to be faced with a group of smiling faces who all started to sing 'Happy birthday to you', as he entered. It was, he realised, 8 February 1974—his twenty-second birthday. Cakes were spread about the decorative table and Ahmad was given a small package. 'Happy birthday,' Wolfgang smiled as he handed it over.

Inside was a booklet, the Gospel of John, written in Arabic. An avid reader who had sorely missed material in his own language, Ahmad began to read as soon as the party was over, his eyes flashing through the pages as he soaked up the story. He told Wolfgang later that day: 'I have had a lot of wrong ideas about Jesus. I thought he was a big prophet and the kind of person you can never understand, but in this book I find he is very easy to understand. His words are simple and he is a real person. I see that he got tired and angry just like I do. But he had mercy on people. In one bit the crowd flung a woman in front of him—she had been caught having an adulterous affair with another man. She deserved to die—that's also the rule in my country. But Jesus had mercy on her and simply told her to go and sin no more.

'I don't understand that—I believe when people have done wrong they deserve to be punished. Perhaps stoning to death is a bit harsh but certainly punishment should be given. But as I read that, I felt tears coming into my eyes; that's the sort of forgiveness I need. I know I have done many wrong things and I am afraid to face God with them. Can Jesus forgive me?'

Despite the assurances of his friend, Ahmad was not really convinced. But as he re-read the book many times he began to see in Jesus Christ something very special.

'I have had heroes, people to look up to,' he pointed out to Wolfgang one evening, 'but they have always let me down. I admired Nasser, the President of Egypt, but he had feet of clay. And the singers who I liked in my country would appear in the newspapers having done bad things. They are no better than me, really. If I am going to have a hero, someone to follow, it has to be someone like this Jesus.'

Despite the growing conviction, however, Ahmad was still finding it difficult to throw off the habits of his past. Newcomers to the mission house who said the wrong thing were put in place by his sharp tongue and occasionally his bunched fists, until a man named Gottfried took one of the meetings. As he finished speaking Ahmad started to question him about Christianity. 'Young man, I don't have a lot of time and I don't want to waste what I have. Do you want to be a Christian, or don't you? Make up your mind.'

Ahmad responded instantly. 'Yes. I am not sure that I can do it or keep it up but I want to try.'

They knelt on the threadbare carpet and Gottfried prayed. Then he invited Ahmad to pray. Ahmad had heard prayers many times in the mission and tried, haltingly, to pray in German. Then he switched languages and in the fluency of his own Arabic began to speak to God. 'I want to believe, but I don't know if this is the right thing for me to do. You will have to make me sure, God,' he prayed. As he did so he felt a surge of emotion like an electric current through his body. He broke down and began to confess all his sins before God; in the process the feeling of warmth and acceptance began to grow on him. He began to feel certain that Jesus Christ was alive, listening, and was the person he needed in his life. 'Thank you for sacrificing yourself for me on the cross—help me to live with you, and die for you,' he prayed.

As he finished the young people of the mission crowded round, tears brimming in their eyes, congratulating him and promising to pray for him. The Lebanese Christian was elated, and for days raided the stocks of mission booklets, using them as he walked the streets of Bremen talking to anyone about his new friend, Jesus. He looked especially for Arabs, trying to express to them the feeling of cleanness and wholeness that had been born in him as he gave himself to Christ. Many regarded him as a Muslim renegade, and others with idle curiosity.

Life was difficult to change, he had developed too many bad habits. But as he told Wolfgang, 'At least I can now tell God I am sorry. I don't want to use it as an excuse, but it is wonderful to know that I am free of those horrible chains of sin that bound me.'

He was given an Arabic Bible and began to read that as avidly as he had pored over the much smaller Gospel of John. The Bible, a dictionary (many of the words were unfamiliar) and Christian books became his constant companions and he also decided to practise the guitar—this was difficult as he had to play left-handed because of the shooting accident which had robbed him of the tips of two fingers on his left hand as a 12-year-old.

Eventually he received his wages from the shipping company and faced the dilemma of what to do. The desire to go back to Lebanon was not so strong now; he wanted to stay with his new Christian friends and learn more about his new faith. But his visa expressly stated that it was valid only for training as a sailor, so he decided reluctantly to try his luck at sea again.

For the next six months he was to sail on three ships—each one a carbon copy of his experiences in the past, except that now it was his religion that made him a lonely man. And his attempts to quench the anger and violence inside him meant that he was victimised more, without the desire to fight back.

But his life at sea ended on board the *Tsar*. Ahmad rejected the advances of girls in port and the temptation to steal and sell liquor and cigarettes, spending his spare time reading the Bible in his cabin. Now he was the one called Jesus. And when one of the sailors caught him reading the Bible at the dining table he roared out to the jeers of the others: 'Why do you read the Bible here? We are Christians and we don't need to read the Bible! Read it in your own cabin.'

Sad at heart Ahmad took his Bible to his cabin and read on, sorry that his companions could not see the deep meaning it gave to life.

The months at sea reinforced his original decision to give up life on board ships, a decision finally completed as the ship gently rocked at anchor in Marseille. Ahmad was eating his breakfast when the captain, a surly aggressive individual, appeared in the doorway.

'You there, Arab, go and paint the funnel.'

'Certainly, sir,' replied Ahmad. 'When I have finished eating. It will only take me a couple of minutes.'

'When I say now, I mean now,' the captain roared.

The captain lurched forward and grasped Ahmad's collar. Ahmad's temper broke. He yanked up a mug of tea and waved it at the captain. 'If you don't leave me alone you'll get this in your face,' he shouted.

Each man stared into the eyes of his opponent. Slipping through the doorway the captain reappeared with an enormous steel soup bowl but as he raised it to strike Ahmad he saw the look in the young man's eyes and backed away, leaving the room.

Ahmad glanced round the room, looking for support. 'I'm entitled to finish my meal, aren't I?' he asked.

'I didn't see what happened,' lied one man. Others merely averted their eyes and began to talk among themselves.

Ahmad had already observed on the voyage the effect of the captain's anger on others who had not been anywhere near as outspoken as he had, and began to fear for his life.

He left the boat and reported to the police, telling them he was afraid of being attacked once the ship left the safety of the French port. They took him to the company representative, a pleasant young man who immediately went with Ahmad and confronted the captain. Furious, the captain signed Ahmad off and returned his passport and seaman's book. The company representative booked him on an aircraft to Bremen, via Paris, and Ahmad made his way back to the mission and the consolation of his friends.

By now he had begun to attend the Evangelical Hohentor Church in Bremen, and poured out his heart to the minister. 'I feel so useless—I need to understand so much more about Christianity and the Bible. Is there a school I can go to?'

The minister looked at him with a smile playing round the corners of his eyes. 'I am travelling to Brocke in the northern Rhinefield to speak at a Bible college next week. You can come with me and speak to the principal.' Ahmad was offered a place, the authorities agreed to alter his visa allowing him to learn theology and, even more miraculous, the church financed the converted Muslim through college for three years.

With war exploding in the Lebanon and his beloved Beirut split by bloodshed and violence, a desire began to grip him to work among foreigners in Bremen. After all, he had come to Christ as a foreigner in a foreign city. He considered the words of a teacher at the Bible college: 'When in doubt about something take a piece of paper and divide it into two columns. On one side write down all the things that seem in favour of the project. On the other side write those things against. When you have done that cross out all the things which you feel are purely selfish—when only the valid items are left you may find the problem solved.' Ahmad took a piece of paper and completed the exercise: he decided to remain in Bremen and work among foreigners.

In 1979 he began. To help him he now had his wife, Rindelt—they had first met when she was a Communist and he was giving out literature in Bremen. Later, at the Jesus Centre, she was converted and once they began working together she supported the two of them on her salary as a teacher.

When she had their first child—named Martin Omar, after Ahmad's father—the church agreed to support them financially and a local Christian Alliance also promised help. Three years later the mission moved into a house in the old cobbled-street part of Bremen with room for meetings, meals, a kitchen, office, and even a room for guests. The office walls are now lined with literature in more than a hundred languages, and messages on cassettes in about sixty.

Life for Ahmad Turkamani is busy—apart from his growing family of three sons, Martin Omar, Christoph Salem, and Peter Ziad. Each week he shares his faith with a growing range of nationalities in the German city, speaking a variety of languages—Arabic, German, English, French and Turkish—in his determination to talk about Jesus Christ, the one who changed his own life so radically.

He still has the Arabic Bible which taught him so many truths in his early Christian days, and the scrap of paper on which he computed his desire to remain in Bremen. One day, when the shooting stops in Lebanon, Ahmad Turkamani may return to share the good news of Christ with his own people; until then he is perfectly satisfied to do it in Europe.

9

Victoria: A housewife's search

When the Second World War struck Europe, Victoria Aberham was just nineteen years old. At the age when most girls of her age in Vienna were enjoying the city's social scene, walking the elegant Kartnerstrasse on Sunday mornings to show off their newest clothes, or simply chatting to boyfriends in the pavement cafés, Victoria was struggling to discover the meaning of life.

Vienna, with its memories of beautiful music, Mozart and Strauss, was to her simply a reflection of the discord she saw all around her.

As a child, born in the slum district of the city, Victoria had been kept awake most nights by the constant whirring and hum of a sewing machine in the room above her; and when that eased it was time for the drunks to stumble and shout their way through the maze of stairways onto which her room backed. When she complained about the sewing machine her unmarried mother simply explained it belonged to a widow who looked after her three children during the day and needed to sew at night to make money on which to live.

An only child, Victoria hardly knew her father, and her mother, a poor woman, constantly wore a shawl to hide the hideous effects of a throat operation which, rather than being successful, had left her with a constant speech impediment so that she could only speak in a whisper.

'Victoria, why does your mother always have a cold?' her friends asked. The youngster got tired of the question, and weary of her stock answer, 'She is not well. Her throat is sore.'

Leaving school at fourteen was a necessity for Victoria; a necessity demanded by the lack of money in the family. She began selling shoes in a shop belonging to her aunt, taking lessons to bolster her inadequate education as and when she could.

Her life became a constant search for meaning and Victoria hunted for answers in whatever corner they could be found. Her mother had a dream book—the so-called meaning of dreams—which was in demand in a neighbourhood where people were too poor to find entertainment in other ways. Victoria's job was to keep track of the book.

'Victoria,' mother would call out. 'I had a dream last night so I need the book; go and find it for me. If you can't bring it back look up fish and goats for me . . .' Victoria traced the book, being read by a neighbour, and checked the index for fish and goats. Then she turned to the respective pages and discovered the numerical value of each as the author had identified it. Those were the key numbers her mother required: they were the clues to interpreting the dream. When the dream was a happy one with a good meaning, life was better for the child. When it was a bad omen, life was hard as Mother sensed doom hanging over her.

'I hate this book,' Victoria would tell her school-friends. There was something evil about it that she could sense just by touching its black cover.

The girl was, however, fascinated by the horo-scopes in newspapers. As often as a newspaper appeared in the house she would eagerly scan the entry under her birth sign to discover her fate over the next few hours, and, having done that, would identify the things that happened and link them with the forecast.

When the fairs came she loved having her fortune told—the fact that it was usually a completely dif-ferent explanation from the previous one didn't seem to matter at all. It was as if life controlled her—and she wanted to know what was to happen in advance, otherwise it was impossible to influ-ence.

So incensed with life was she that one day, in a fit of depression and pique, she visited an older friend who, at nearly fifty, was in an even worse state. The pair agreed that, because life wasn't worth living, they would end it. Their suicide pact took them into the woman's bathroom where Victoria carefully switched on the gas water heater without igniting the gas. As the jet sprayed its deadly fumes into the small room with a gentle soothing sound she lay on the concrete floor, her head cushioned by a neatly folded towel as if it would take the sting out of death.

Suddenly the friend, realising the enormity of what they were doing, switched off the gas and grabbed Victoria's ankles, dragging her from the room. 'I can't go through with it,' she wept. Together their tears merged in mutual acceptance: they both felt useless and even death was beyond them. Walking back to her home Victoria was sick in the street; the nausea of her experience was just too much.

The opportunity to marry came as a relief; an attractive girl, Victoria was desperate to escape the poverty-trap of home life and enjoy some of the pleasures she saw others around her engaged in. Her sole pleasures had been dubious ones: she was born, it seemed, with a temperament that encouraged her to break laws. 'Why should men make laws?' was her constant question at school. 'What right have they to dictate to the rest of us?' She lied, stole, and eventually went to bed with the man who was to become her husband in a devil-may-care demonstration of her lack of concern for the rules of society.

It was in August 1939 at the age of nineteen that she was married to Ludwig Seibel. He was a salesman who sold stretchers for shoes. At first the upright man, twenty-six years her senior, seemed to have the answers for which she was seeking. Their first meeting, on a bench in a park, had sparked off discussions, and when Victoria discovered he had studied philosophy at school she felt magnetised by him.

They would talk for hours about the great philosophers of the past and Victoria would dream of the day when she could begin to spend time studying their work: 'I'm certain it holds the key to life itself,' she told her husband. It certainly held the key to as discordant a future as she had a past.

For the young woman rejected the thought of working in a factory, which was the general rule for women as the war blazed across Europe, deciding instead to have a family—one of the few guarantees by which a woman could stay at home. By the age of twenty, Eva was born, and eighteen months later Othmar, with Alexander following eighteen months on again.

Life was hectic and full of troubles. Her interest in the future and astrology was one of the few things that kept her sane. But as she settled into life with her husband there were compensations: he had a good job and Victoria began to enjoy the luxuries of life. They were living in a better area of the city, Breitenfurt, although that house didn't come to them easily. Because their home was in the sector of Austria under Russian occupation after the war, they were unable to move straight into it. But Victoria and Ludwig knew the woman who had been put in charge of the house, and eventually managed to talk her into allowing them to rent a room in their own house! Eventually the Russians left and the house was returned to them—but only after they had paid another nominal price for its return.

It was, however, Victoria's astute mind that led to them getting a second house at a very low cost—in her own name.

Ludwig was a good salesman—but was not so good as a debt collector. He was often owed money and was too easygoing, too philosophical to demand payment; when he did, he invariably lost the inevitable court case. But the couple found a plot of land on the north-east bank of the Danube that was ideal for the house Victoria wanted built—

it was also very cheap because it was land owned by a monastery. The monks were afraid their Russian overlords would seize it during the occupation, so sold it in plots at vastly reduced prices, anxious to get what they could rather than lose everything. The plot which the young couple purchased included a partly-built house.

'We can't afford to finish the building,' Ludwig pointed out. Victoria began to forage through his business books. 'Look here, that carpenter owes you a lot of money, what do you intend to do?' she quizzed.

'I'll probably take him to court if he doesn't pay up,' said her husband.

'Yes, and lose like you always do. No, this time let me handle it.'

Victoria dialled the number on the telephone and spoke to the builder. 'You have this rather large debt outstanding,' she pointed out. 'My husband would like it settled and is thinking of going to court over the matter.' When she had established that the builder was concerned, she went on: 'But I have an idea to save us all the trouble—and save you a lot of money. We have just bought a plot of land in the city which includes a house that needs quite a bit of rebuilding. We think that the outstanding work is well within the price of your debt and wonder if you would like to finish off the house. That way you will save money and we shall save the trouble of having to take you to court and engaging legal advisers.'

The offer was accepted; the house was completed—a useful second home for the family of five.

Victoria enjoyed living in the better area—and made a number of influential friends, one being a woman who specialised in holding parties at which a spiritist medium would hold seances. Victoria went to several of the meetings, enjoying the feel of the luxurious furniture, and meeting fascinating people—including a well-known author of children's books and important local dignitaries.

And Victoria's confidence was boosted when the medium, during a particular trance, called to her that she had a picture of her past life. 'I see you, my dear, thousands of years ago—a beautiful Greek maiden. Your name is Pallas-Athene, the daughter of the god Zeus . . .' she was told. Outside the Parliament building in Vienna, a thirteen-foot high statue of Pallas-Athene stood, and she had long admired the beautiful Greek goddess with a gilded helmet, armed with a lance—now she learned it was merely her in a previous existence. 'I feel it could be true,' Victoria confided to her friends. 'Anything is possible and this medium has told us many things that appear to be true. In any case, it is better to believe in that than nothing.'

A previous effort at reaching the spirit world had ended in failure. Then she had been invited to a house where the guests sat round a circular table and laid their hands on the table asking it to move any number of times according to the question. 'We asked it to move the number of years that would take place before the war ended; it didn't move. I was so disappointed,' Victoria had complained. Others had told her the table had revealed the times of different events to them—in years and months.

As the children grew older, and were all at school, Victoria realised the dream she had long held: she decided to go to university. First she had to do a three-year course to finish off the education which had been reduced by her health and the necessity to work. This course—it actually took her four years—was to earn her the entry qualifications for university.

She began to love school and learning. The mornings were spent in the school to enable her to return home before the children arrived. 'Learning is not a thing requiring intelligence—just endurance,' her teacher told her with a grin. Victoria smiled and endured. She disciplined herself to get through the work and at night when she could not sleep—her childhood insomnia problem proved impossible to break—she reached to the side of the bed for her study books. Her goal was definite: a place at university.

Her studies were conducted while she surrounded herself with other problems of a more personal nature. Now thirty-nine, Victoria had tired of life with Ludwig and decided to leave him, packing her suitcases and moving from the home in Breitenfurt into which they had moved, to the house in Vienna which had been built at her suggestion.

A flat in the country—Wieselburg—had introduced her to another man, Friedrich Aberham; another salesman, who sold tables to furniture dealers. They had known each other for some time—Friedrich's grandmother was a friend of Victoria, living in the same block of flats—and, meeting him while walking one day, Victoria decided that he was the man who would offer her the new life she sought. The culminating factor in her decision to leave Ludwig came when the couple were in the car and he drove it into a tree. With a cut across her scalp, Victoria was suddenly tired of the arguments and frustrations of their lives together, and wanted a change. Friedrich promised the fresh inspiration for that future.

She moved back to Vienna and concluded her school course with the necessary qualifications for university—ironically starting at the same time as her eldest son, Othmar, and sitting next to him in some of the classes. Victoria was studying philosophy with history and art as secondary subjects. At forty she was the oldest in the class but that didn't concern her: learning did.

Her leather bag was packed with the tools of her studies—demonstrated when she dropped it one day as the tram on which she was travelling lurched round a corner of the ring circling the Inner Stadt. Pens, pencils, geometry instruments, rulers and books tumbled out on to the floor. 'For a lady you certainly have an unusual range of items in your bag,' remarked a man politely as he laughingly bent to help pick up the items strewn around.

Philosophy was taken in the institute building in the centre of Vienna—the old university, where the seats were ranged in tiers around the central lecture platform. Victoria hung on the words of the professors, anxious to pull aside the veil which seemed always to shimmer between her intellect and the great questions which buzzed in her mind.

She began to consider the implications of the great thinkers of the past: Socrates, named as the wisest man in Athens in his day, 400 BC; Aristotle the third-century BC Greek philosopher, pupil of Plato and tutor of Alexander the Great; Thomas

Aquinas, the Dominican and Italian scholastic philosopher of the thirteenth century . . .; but the one who took her attention was St Augustine, the fourth-century Numidian churchman and Christian convert. As her lecturer, a short, clean-shaven man, got into the story of Augustine, she became excited. The professor made the one-time Bishop of Hippo in North Africa live.

The lecture ended with the professor, having outlined the life of St Augustine, promising to return the following week with the great man's message. 'I'm sure this is what I have been searching for,' Victoria confessed to a friend during the morning break. 'I have the feeling that our next session will contain all the answers to life. I really can't wait.'

But the following week brought disappointment. Somehow the enthusiasm and excitement of seven days ago was gone; the message was interesting, but not as challenging as Victoria had dared hope. 'Just when I thought the truth was coming, it doesn't,' she wept as she returned home to the daily drudge of housework. 'Why does life have to be so disappointing? Why are its answers so elusive?'

Her lectures posed more problems than they presented answers. The great men of the past, she discovered, offered few realities; instead they created more enigmas in her alert mind. She was content with the message of Augustine alone, but it lacked dynamic, anything to change her life.

Victoria's acute distress had its effects in other parts of her life.

As her final year at university arrived (she was now forty-seven) Victoria needed to unclutter her mind to write the dissertation that would, she hoped, earn her the degree for which she had worked. Two more children, Gudrun and Mathias, had slowed down her university studies, but she was determined to eventually succeed.

By then her new husband had had another house built—just fifty yards from Victoria's own home. A beautiful, spacious residence in the same quiet road, just a two-minute walk from the tram-line, it was sheltered with walnut and horse-chestnut trees. Her former home was to be given to Alexander, the youngest son by her first husband, but in the meantime Victoria decided to rent it out on a short-term basis.

An advertisement brought a young American to her door. Greg Livingstone explained that he was looking for a building to rent for a Christian organisation called Operation Mobilisation. They were mostly young people but would look after the house. Victoria took a liking to the earnest young man and agreed to allow OM to have the building. But they wouldn't be able to occupy it for another three months. She was perplexed: it was hard to find someone wanting to rent for such a short time. Later the same day an agency telephoned: they had three couples, all musicians staying at the Intercontinental Hotel, who wanted a place for just three months—was there any chance?

Three months later the young people from OM moved in. They invited Victoria to sit with them any day as they had their morning Bible study and prayer time. Because it was vacation time at the university she decided to look in on the first meeting to discover the calibre of the youngsters who were using her home.

As the group of a dozen sat in a circle she was given a Bible—the first time in her life she had seen one, despite some unsuccessful visits to a Roman Catholic church as a child. Victoria's pulse raced as she read the book for the first time; she knew immediately that the forty-seven years she had spent studying philosophy, searching for meaning in life, were almost over—this book had the answers. Despite the fact that the Bible was in English, her stumbling use of that language enabled her to feel and sense the awesome discoveries she would find within its pages. The group turned to the Gospel of John, chapter three, and Victoria read of how a religious man, searching for truth, had made a midnight visit to Jesus Christ to pose the same sort of eternal questions she had been asking.

The man, Nicodemus, had recognised in Jesus a man of authority—'you must have been sent by God to do the things you do,' he told Jesus. But Jesus didn't get embroiled in the leader's assessment; instead he came directly to the point: 'You can't see the kingdom of God unless you are born again.'

Victoria's eyes raced across the unfamiliar language as she puzzled over the same problem that Nicodemus had faced two thousand years before. 'How can a man be born again when he is old?' Nicodemus asked Jesus.

Patiently Jesus answered: 'A person is born physically of human parents, but he is born spiritually of the Spirit.'

The small group began to discuss the passage, talking easily and freely about how each person in turn had become a Christian by being born again.

As she walked the few yards back to her own home Victoria felt elated: somehow she now understood the mystery for which she had been searching—she needed to be born again. She knelt and prayed to God asking for the new birth, the new life that comes only through Jesus Christ entering a person's life and giving a fresh start. She stumbled over the sins she could recall from her past, confessing them to God and asking for forgiveness, feeling as she did so, a lightning of her spirit.

Subsequent conversations with the OM young people encouraged her. 'In just one second I knew that the Bible contained the truth and that the truth was encompassed in one person, Jesus Christ,' she told Greg. 'I knew I only had to identify with Jesus Christ to be free. Now I am so happy.'

Friedrich, used to his wife's philosophical interludes, accepted her new faith phlegmatically. 'It's a fresh hobby—it will pass' he thought to himself. But he began to realise that it was not as simple as that when he noticed that Victoria was putting God first in everything she did; the Bible studies were now a vital part of her life; university was forgotten and the dissertation which would have enabled her to gain her degree was still only seventeen pages long—forgotten and ignored.

Nine months later he made the same step, and became a Christian.

It was a moment of great joy to Victoria. She had recognised that her divorce was wrong, her life had been wasted; all the mistakes from her past poured out like a flood as she considered them, along with God, and she admitted that she could do nothing about them. They were in the past. But as she prayed, asking for forgiveness, she felt the soothing ointment of the Holy Spirit being applied to her soul; peace came for the first time in her life.

Victoria read the Bible avidly, to make up for her forty-seven lost years. The years of study at school and university had equipped her to make every moment count—including the hours during the nights when she could not sleep. Unable to find a church in which she felt comfortable, she began to invite local children into her own home to be taught Christianity, alongside those of her own children still living at home, Gudrun and Mathias. Mathias was six years old, and many of his school-friends began to accept the invitation to attend Sunday school in his home. Children were soon making decisions for Christ and Victoria was anxious to reach the parents also.

The quick-thinking mind that had worked out the system to buy and build the house now used by OM, also concocted a way to reach the mothers. Her home had a sauna alongside the basement room in which she taught the children, so Victoria invited the mothers: 'Don't just drop the children off when you bring them to Sunday school—come in as well, use the sauna while I speak to the children and then, afterwards, we can have tea together.' Once several mothers had agreed it was easy. They sat swathed in towels in the sauna and Victoria took their children in the adjacent large room—speaking extra loudly so that her voice was carried into the sauna. Afterwards mothers asked about God and Victoria saw some become Christians too.

For five years she enjoyed attending the OM Bible studies before one of its leaders, Ed Paterson, from Canada, decided to begin a small church in the area. Ed launched the church with Victoria and her husband as two of the first members; now, ten years later, there are more than a hundred adults and forty children in the church. Victoria has helped in the Sunday school for years—as well as joining others in sharing their faith on the city streets. For two hours every Saturday evening the police allow the church to hold a meeting on the Karntner Strasse, a key street corner in the area. Her eldest son Othmar—one of the church elders— is the main speaker, Mathias speaks and plays the guitar and Friedrich has also shared his faith on the street as well as being a gifted speaker in church.

Victoria likes nothing better than to give the testimony of how God met her: she's done it all over Austria, in Scotland and France.

The most moving occasion, however, was when she visited her father shortly after her conversion. Curiosity had led her, when she was sixteen years old, to discover where he was living and she had occasionally visited him and his wife. But when she became a Christian (her mother had died) she insisted on telling her father her story. She read from the Bible, explaining the encounter of Jesus and Nicodemus just as she had first heard it. Eight years later, when her father was eighty-six, he became a Christian and told his daughter: 'I think back on my whole life and see all the wrong I have done. I wanted to do the right things but couldn't. Now I know the devil was pushing me into the wrong way continually.' Victoria could only weep with joy. At his funeral, his grandchild Othmar preached at the graveside. Victoria regularly visited her father's second wife, doing her shopping each week, and within three years of the death of her husband she too became a Christian.

Now sixty-seven, Victoria, a small, active woman, has changed her philosophical view of life. 'I know the real truth of the words in the Bible, "If anyone is in Christ he is a new creature. The old is gone; lo, the new has come," (2 Corinthians 5:17) because it happened to me. His love wraps round me like a blanket now, sheltering me securely. I discovered that Jesus said, "I am the truth"—it was the truth for which I was searching, and I found it not in the great philosophers of the past but in the person of Jesus Christ. Life is not dull any longer; with Jesus each day is exciting and an adventure.'

10

Stuart: No fighting God!

With a crash the window shattered. Glass tinkled on to the stone floor. The three youths stood poised, listening to see whether or not the noise had been heard. When they were confident no one had reacted 16-year-old Stuart McAllister, the ringleader, prised away the remaining shards from the frame and pulled himself through the opening. He walked cautiously across the factory floor, pausing every few feet to make sure he was still the only occupier of the building on the outskirts of Glasgow.

Stealthily he reached the place where he knew the side door to be, twisted back the bolt and pulled the door open just wide enough for his companions to enter.

Stuart repeated the plan to them: then nodded and led them to the two huge 500-gallon tanks of paraffin on one side of the works area. Used to clean spare parts, the fuel was stored in the metal drums, a valve near the base giving access. Stuart turned the lever on the nearest container; the liquid poured out with a steady trickle. He leapt aside as it quickly gathered momentum and soaked the area on which he had been standing, and twisted towards the second drum, opening that tap in similar fashion. Again he had to move smartly to avoid having the fuel splash his scruffy shoes.

Working by the crisp light of the moon that beamed through the wide windows set high in the walls, the trio watched as the paraffin filtered its way across the floor, leaving two huge tractor units on a small island and then eating its way to their bases. A row of new lawn mowers, ranged along one side of the factory floor, were soon engulfed in the spreading fuel. Within minutes the whole area was swimming inches deep, the acrid smell filling the youngsters' nostrils as it mingled with the stench of paint stripper and oil.

'Let's get out,' Stuart called and his accomplices needed no second warning. Quickly they left by the door, which had been left on the latch. There was just one more thing Stuart wanted to do before they completed the night's work and ran into the safety of the darkness. With the door slightly ajar he flicked a cigarette lighter and held it under a piece of paper snatched from the office on the way out. It flared in his hand; he threw it through the gap, slamming the iron door to and scurried off as fast as he could.

In the privacy of his home Stuart lay on his bed, his hands behind his head, smiling grimly to himself. 'That will show them. They're not dealing with the factory boy now,' he mused.

He considered the posters in the room he shared with his older brother—Raquel Welch scantily clad in a fur bikini running from a prehistoric monster in the film *2000 Years BC*, and the white-faced David Bowie, and Heavy Metal's Alice Cooper stared back at him. For Stuart life was as violent as the bounding rock music he enjoyed, and the thrill of subterfuge was exciting. He leaned forward and lifted open the desk-top on the record sleeve of his latest Alice Cooper record; a pair of girl's knickers were revealed. He chuckled to himself; it was the sort of bizarre motif that appealed to him. He was glad his brother was a habitual late-night owl. He had a few more minutes to gloat over tonight's exercise of revenge.

It was the nasty side of his character that had led Stuart into trouble with the police months before. That incident ended with a police officer, who believed he could be rehabilitated, getting him a job with a friend who ran the factory into which he had broken earlier that evening. The job was to give Stuart a new start in life: instead the youngster hated the oily stench and dirty, junior jobs that came his way.

Conceived into a violent environment in Glasgow, he had enjoyed the fear of gang fights, the sight of graffiti, and the whimpering of the weak as they were threatened and beaten by the bully-boys. For Stuart McAllister life promised to be one long brush with the law.

He had enjoyed his early teenage life on the east side of the city, slipping easily into the gangland atmosphere despite the fact that, with middle-class parents, he stuck out like a sore thumb. After a youth had been stabbed in his own street Stuart's parents had begun to get concerned for the well-being of their son and moved to a better part of the city—a true middle-class environment. It was a terrible wrench for the youngster. The adjustment to new friends and a new way of life was too much. He already had a negative view of his father and the tension between the two grew. Father—a buyer with a large retail company dealing in men's clothes—humiliated the boys, lecturing them on their misdemeanours and trying to pressure them into developing clever brains. Because his father admired intellectuals Stuart grew up hating academics and any form of reading and intellectual exercise.

The best fighter in his class, he continually picked fights and when the family moved, his frustration at the new environment showed itself in the development of new, more violent, friendships, vandalism, and drinking. A night spent smashing car windows, or breaking up bus shelters, would end with bottles of spirits and beer.

One night he was carried home from the pub by a friend—drunk despite being under age. As he came to on the doorstep Stuart was desperate to get to his own room before his parents saw the state he was in, but as he stumbled over the threshold the noise he made gave his presence away and he crashed into the stairs, unable to climb. As his mother helped him to his room she discovered the motor cycle chain he wore as a belt and the flick-knife that nestled against his side. She was horrified, and as the burly boy struggled to free himself from her grasp she ran next door to get help until Father returned.

When Stuart's father appeared he walked briskly into the bedroom, looked at his son, still dazed, lying on the bed, and promised that the next day he would take photographs of the boy to every pub in the district and threaten the landlords that if they served him again, under age, they would be taken to court. Stuart's anger burst out. 'I hate you,' he shouted. 'I want to get out of this prison and join the army.' Father stared at him, stone-faced, and replied: 'Fine, go ahead. See if they can make a man of you.'

The next day Stuart walked into the army recruiting office in Glasgow, eyeing the posters on the walls exhibiting the different branches of the services. The marines looked appealing—the uniforms and muscular men seemed to have a particularly attractive life-style. It was, however, not to be. 'Sorry son,' the officer told him. 'You're too young. Come back in a couple of years' time.'

The disgruntled youngster left school and began working in a local supermarket as a box boy, carrying cardboard boxes packed with groceries to customers' cars, running errands and helping clean up the store. The £6.50 he earned seemed to go nowhere: £4 went straight to his mother and the remaining £2.50 was squandered away on drink and entertainment—all gone by Saturday night.

And Stuart was not free of the tempestuous background which had encouraged his parents to move house years before. His drinking fuelled the fires of violence, and he was soon involved in vandalism which led to his first brush with the law. Taken to court after smashing a telephone kiosk Stuart was one of the few middle-class youngsters in the street gang. One of the police officers took him to one side. 'You can do better than this, son,' he said. 'I want to help you. You don't want to let your parents down. Give me a few days and I'll see if I can get you a job—something to give you a fresh start where they won't ask questions.'

The officer was as good as his word and a couple of days later turned up at the house to tell Stuart to report to the factory the following Monday. 'The boss is a friend of mine and they will look after you and teach you a trade. Take advantage of this; it's good of them to give you a job, there are a lot of kids out of work,' the officer added.

A rebellion against any sort of authority showed itself with that first skirmish with the police, and their well-meaning efforts at reform which had got him the job at the factory as an apprentice, mending tractors and lawn mowers, had proved little inspiration to change his ways. The factory do-everything boy, Stuart's hatred of the place and his menial life finally led him to break in and attempt to set fire to the whole factory. When he had left in such a hurry he had believed that with all the fumes that were in the air the sheet of flaming paper must almost have caused an explosion. Certainly there would be little of the factory left by morning.

But when he returned to work the following day, casually pretending nothing was different, he discovered everything the same; men working, and the heavy pungent smell of paraffin in the air. A couple of police officers were wandering among the earlier arrivals chatting and making notes.

Stuart couldn't believe the place was still standing: there had been enough paraffin to have ripped it apart. He was never to discover why the flaming paper didn't cause the havoc he had intended. And even though he was questioned closely and the manager who had originally given him the job watched him constantly throughout the day, he was never openly accused. He knew, deep down, however, that they suspected him. Later that day the 16-year-old walked from the building and told the boss he wouldn't be back. 'I've had enough of this place,' he called. 'Don't expect to see me again. Send my cards to my home.'

At home Stuart's parents were not enthusiastic about their son's decision to quit. Confrontations with his father became more regular and his drinking increased also. Stuart was to get rid of the thick Doc Martin-style bovver boots, his Crombie coats, the chain-belt and other trappings of thuggery, thanks to his next job. Now reaching the age of seventeen he tried life behind the counter in a men's boutique. Snappy, sharp clothes became the order of the day and while he was changing his dress he began to alter other aspects of his life. Drink was still a major hazard in his life but girls were proving to be equally as attractive, as he desperately searched for something to lift him above his peers.

His weekly earnings had soared since the factory days—he was the shop's best salesman when sober. One drunken day, however, he got his orders from his father: 'I want you out, son. We can't put up with any more behaviour like this.'

It suited Stuart. He had already had exploratory talks with a friend about renting a flat between them; now it could actually happen. He had soon got his own room—no sharing with an older brother; Bruce Lee posters dominated the wall as a tribute to his latest craze—karate. He joined a karate club, which only accentuated the violent life that was becoming second nature to the tough city kid.

His sales technique was making him rich among his companions and he was also asked to work in the local dance hall—Shuffles. 'What doing?' Stuart asked.

'Not a lot,' was the reply. 'We need another bouncer, someone to get rid of the folk we don't want in. There will be a bit of fighting, you can dance, meet the girls, and get paid for it.'

Not only was it easy work but Stuart rapidly began to enjoy the violent side of the trade. Shuffles was a huge dance-hall with up to 2,500 people, the biggest bands and music groups, and a lot of opportunities for anyone with a violent streak in his nature. Not only that: his working partner was also named Stuart—Big Stuart, because of his bulk—and the two soon became inseparable in and out of fights. Big Stuart and Little Stuart were the team to be feared, the men you called on if you wanted someone hurt, and they had few scruples. Stuart had begun weight-lifting three times a week—power-lifting to give him extra strength—and his colleague was fond of tall stories, so it was a friendship that clicked.

One evening a group of sailors arrived with the intention of taking the dance-hall by storm: they had not known about Big Stuart and Little Stuart. While his fellow-tars were nursing their injuries after a fracas the leader clung to the door-frame of the dance-hall's entrance to prevent the Stuarts from carrying him into the rear of the hall to work him over. Stuart couldn't relax the huge sailor's grip and so grabbed a fire extinguisher from its base besides the door, smashed it against the sailor's hand; and, as his knuckles cracked, his screams were drowned by the two men dragging him bodily to a back room where he was beaten. A fracture of the skull, broken jaw, and a number of smashed ribs were an expensive price to play for his night of entertainment.

The two Stuarts fled north to escape the police, taking jobs in Inverness on a construction site working on the floating bells that were used to take North Sea oil rigs out to sea. It was tough hard work but Stuart, who had lied about his age telling them he was eighteen, a year older than he actually was, loved it—and the £100-plus a week that went with it. The enormous wage paid for the couple to spend their free time lazing in the best hotels in the Aviemore Centre where they lived like rich lords, enjoying the sporting facilities, the friendship of women, and drinking—always drinking.

Four months later Big Stuart was tracked down by the police and required as a witness and Stuart, now lonely, decided to return home. He lived with his parents for a while but his father still couldn't cope with his son's truculence, and Stuart was soon up to his old tricks, working in another dance-hall, enjoying the scraps, and looking for action.

He found the extra action after a visit from a tall, burly character to the hall one evening. Monty, a one-time boxer, one of Glasgow's shady characters, was a likeable man whose size and skill with his fists had earned him the job of bodyguard for some of the country's sporting personalities. 'How would you like to work for me?' he quizzed Stuart during a lull in the dance-hall. Monty mentioned the second-hand car business he owned and the work sounded interesting, as well as the opportunity to be seen alongside one of the area's best-known personalities.

The job entailed Stuart cleaning cars and delivering them to clients. It was fortunate, he realised, that while working in Inverness he had troubled to learn how to drive the vans on the site and, without a licence, he soon found himself at the wheel of a sparkling range of vehicles which enhanced his reputation further and attracted the attention of the girls. Monty began to appreciate his new employee: 'I want someone who I can trust—who's untrustworthy, if you understand what I mean,' he explained. 'You seem willing to keep your mouth shut and look after my interests when I'm away from the business. You can count on me looking after you,' he promised.

Stuart moved into his own luxury two-bedroomed penthouse with a large lounge kitted out with leather, padded swivel-armchairs, an enormous leather sofa, red plush carpet, and a large-screen television in a walnut cabinet.

Life was reaching the pinnacle he had long striven for. He would park a large Jaguar or Mercedes outside his parent's home, invite his pert, attractive 24-year-old girl-friend Joyce—six years his senior—to meet his parents and flaunt the wealth he was acquiring before his father's cynical eyes. 'I just want money—you can get anything with money,' he said to Joyce in a moment of closeness. At last he appeared to be reaching the goals he had set for himself.

It was Joyce who began to break the hint of perfection when she announced one evening: 'I must tell you, Stuart, I've seen another guy. He's the fellow who was giving me driving lessons; he asked me for a date and I agreed—I don't know why. I don't love him. I just love you and wanted you to know.'

Stuart went berserk. He flung a vase across the room, grabbed Joyce by the arm and dragged her across to him. 'You slag,' he shouted. 'Get out of here—and don't come back.'

She tried to explain that it was a one-night stand that meant nothing, but Stuart was not even listening. He was dragging clothes from the wardrobe and flinging them on to the floor. 'Get out . . .'

As she gathered up her belongings Stuart stormed out, leapt in his car and crashed the accelerator to the floor as it surged on its way. Stuart screeched to a halt outside the motoring school and barged through the glass-fronted door. 'You, out here,' he said, motioning to the instructor who sat with others drinking tea. The instructor put down his cup, puzzled, and made for the door. As it closed behind him Stuart muttered: 'You've been seeing my girl-friend I hear?'

'What of it? It's one of those things. You don't own her.'

Without another word Stuart smashed his elbow into the man's face, rammed his fist into his stomach and as the victim crashed to the floor kicked and punched him, all the while screaming, 'Perhaps that will teach you to leave my women alone in future.'

Other instructors poured from the office, mouths agape, watching the uneven struggle. Stuart looked

up—'Want to fight?'—and as they refused his challenge, leapt back into his car and drove off.

At Cranston Hill police station in the centre of
Glasgow officers angrily tried to get Stuart to confess to the assault. 'I know nothing about it,' he
maintained. 'Ask him if it was me. If you've got
evidence—prove it. If not, I want to go.' His
demands for a lawyer were unheard but eventually
he walked from the station knowing that he had
won his case: no charges were to be pressed.

Three days later a confused Stuart took Joyce
back. He knew he wanted her company but could
not understand the events of life: just as he seemed
to be getting on top something else happened to
knock him down.

Trouble seemed to dog his footsteps. City life,
which had hardened his life-style, was keeping it
tough. Another tough year of frenzied activity in the
garage, the dance-hall and fluctuating relationships
with Joyce culminated in an incident which threatened his liberty. Alec, a friend who owned a garage,
telephoned to ask for help. He had been selling
trucks as new—they were actually reconditioned
models and most had had very little recondi-
tioning —but one man was refusing to pay. Alec
needed the money. Stuart went along to help.

The argument got heated and Alec, a former
boxer, punched the customer, who crashed to the
ground, dead! Alec was arrested and Stuart was
absolutely thrilled to be connected with a murder
case—a key witness. He claimed that the man had
fallen and banged his head on the car and Alec
escaped with a year in prison for manslaughter.
During the trial the Procurator Fiscal ordered

Stuart into a side room along with police officers to warn him, 'You are a compulsive liar. I am advising the police to put you in prison if you don't begin to tell the truth.' Only the threat of involving a skilful lawyer helped Stuart off the hook.

Back in his luxury flat, considering the case, Stuart began to think that life might get back to something approaching its violent norm until Joyce returned one evening and popped him a strange question. 'What do you think about Jesus Christ?' she asked.

Stuart's grandmother had been a Christian but that was as near as Stuart had ever got to church-going. He despised it as an activity for little old ladies—and kids who couldn't fight back. He had read Erich von Daniken's book, *Chariots of the Gods*, and explained to Joyce that Jesus was simply someone from another planet, a mysterious being who had amazed people by his superior intellect and ability. He certainly wasn't anyone to get worked up over. 'It was just that people thought he was God because he was so advanced,' he claimed.

The next day Joyce came home from work with a Bible, a gift from a Roman Catholic girl who had started getting her interested in God. Joyce began to ask questions continually about God, Jesus and the Bible. She finally made her way to a Baptist church and arrived back to tell Stuart, 'I've become a Christian. I've given my life to Jesus Christ and I feel wonderful.'

'Don't talk daft, woman. It's a phase. You'll get over it. They've just brainwashed you.'

'Not at all. Jesus has washed my sins away with his blood—but no one has brainwashed me.'

'What a load of rubbish,' Stuart snorted, leaving the house for the dance-hall. Joyce's next move shook him even more: she announced she was leaving the flat. 'Now I am a Christian I realise it is wrong for us to live together—I'm still married to my husband, after all. I'm moving out and going to live with a friend.'

Stuart grew frantic. The few previous weeks without Joyce had convinced him he needed her companionship. He tried desperately to convince her that she was wrong, religion was wrong, moving away was wrong; she dithered between the persuasive arguments he put up, and the even more convincing views of her new Christian friends. Several times Stuart practically forced her into bed with him and, smothering her with sex and stimulation tried to drive the religious thoughts from her.

Joyce almost had a nervous breakdown, so tremendous was the pressure on her, until eventually she left. As she packed her suitcases Stuart ranted on: 'Get out, then, and don't come back. I never want to see you again. You're crazy.'

But the one who was the more crazy was Stuart himself, picking fights to keep his mind from concentrating on his social life, and driving his Capri 2000GT at 70 miles per hour through the city in the hope the police would stop him and give him the excuse for a punch-up.

Life was worse than ever—and he missed Joyce terribly, more than he would dare admit to her, his friends or even to himself. When she did suggest they spent an evening together he agreed, thinking it would be easy to talk her into returning. They met in the city but Stuart discovered that Joyce only wanted to talk to him about becoming a Christian. 'Stuart,' she gabbled, 'It is a marvellous life. It is what you need. Jesus is the one to give you a new start. He can do it for you, just like he has for me. Please try . . .'

Her pleading fell on deaf ears but he finally agreed to go for tea with her to two of her new friends. 'Then you can get lost and take Jesus with you,' he threatened.

They drove to the house, an ordinary semi-detached in one of the middle-class areas of the city. As Stuart followed Joyce up the short path he began to sense something unusual. And as the door opened and the couple welcomed them, kissing Joyce and shaking his hand, the tenseness he was already feeling became worse. Ushered into the sitting-room, the very atmosphere seemed one of peace and serenity, something Stuart was not used to, and he perched on the edge of the seat, uncomfortable and not knowing how to handle himself. Soft music played what he heard to be Christian songs in the background and he instantly noticed that there was no dominating television in the room—it really was different.

George and Elsie, the couple, began to talk about how much Jesus had changed their lives and Joyce occasionally chipped in to agree. Elsie, a vivacious personality, giggled when he brought up his space-man theory and George immediately shot it down in flames. They read passages from the Bible that seemed to burn into his mind; he was beginning to see the reality of what they were talking about. As the conversation moved on to the second coming of Jesus—when, as George explained, Jesus returns to

collect those who are Christians before finally ending the world as it is and establishing the new
heaven—Stuart considered his own past, the fights,
damage, lies—'Could Jesus take me?' he asked.
And, answering the question in his own mind, he
added, 'Not as I am. I'm too bad.'

George and Elsie stood and left to go to the
kitchen to prepare tea and as soon as they had gone
Joyce, sensing a moment of truth, looked Stuart in
the eyes and said: 'Well, are you going to do anything about it? Do you want to be a Christian?'

Stuart didn't answer. Instead he shrugged his
shoulders and uncurled himself from the chair,
making his way to the bathroom. As he pressed
home the latch on the bathroom door he began to
sob, knelt on the pink carpet alongside the pink
bath and prayed for the first time in his life. 'I do
want to be a Christian, Jesus. What do I have to
do? Is it really as simple as they were saying, just
asking you to take away my sin and live in me? If it
is, please do it. I want to get rid of the dirty things
in my life and be new.'

He felt instantly better. Relief and reality flooded
into his heart. Stuart knew something had happened. He walked down the stairs to be met by
three sets of eyes staring at him with open questions
written in them. 'What have you done?' asked
Joyce.

'I have prayed and asked the Lord Jesus into my
life,' was the muttered reply.

The trio began laughing, crying, and scrambled
across the room to all hug him at once. 'What have
I got myself into?' he questioned.

As the laughter subsided George suggested
prayer, so all four knelt in a circle on the floor. 'I

hope I've come to you for the right reason,' prayed Stuart. 'I don't think it was because I wanted Joyce back—I don't know, but you do.'

In his flat that evening Stuart was suddenly aware of just how temporal and temporary were the trappings of luxury that surrounded him; he began to appreciate the peace and joy that came from simply knowing he was a Christian and at peace with God. 'I feel different, as if I am a new person. I know that somehow things are going to be different,' he told his amazed mother. The next day Mother returned from the shops with a black, zip-sided Bible. 'I hope that helps,' she told him.

Stuart moved back into his parents' house, despite Father's scepticism, but couldn't raise the courage to tell his workmates about his new life. When Joyce visited him at the garage she would boldly talk about Jesus to Monty and the salesmen, leaving Stuart embarrassed, and his embarrassment grew worse when she left and his mates told ribald stories about her and about God.

Stuart was now a director of the garage, having been Monty's close companion for some years, but even his elevated status couldn't get him the week off he wanted when Joyce suggested they both went on a missionary camp. However, Monty appeared one day to announce one of his frequent trips away from the garage had been cancelled—it was the week of the camp, so Stuart was able to take the week off after all.

The camp was in a picturesque school in the middle of a forest on the west coast of Scotland. The two key speakers both impressed Stuart; Dr Alex Scott and Jonathan McRostie, European Director

of Operation Mobilisation. They both made the
Christian life sound real and dynamic and challenged those at the camp to do something worthwhile with their lives. Stories of Christian martyrs,
like Jim Elliot, killed by the remote South American
Auca Indians to whom he had gone to preach,
excited Stuart's love of adventure. Christianity, he
realised, was something worth telling others about.

He was challenged in other areas also. He was
passing by a small group studying the Bible on one
occasion and heard them talking about divorce.
Stopping to listen, he heard them discuss Christian
marriage and how the Bible advocated one man-
one woman for life. It stunned him: Stuart had
fondly imagined that Joyce would eventually get a
divorce and that the two of them would marry and
settle down. This new insight made that seem
impossible. Joyce got involved in the conversation
too and he could see the doubt and pain registering
on her.

Talking to one of the leaders afterwards they
explained their position and were advised to separate for a while 'to see if God will show you what is
best'. Never one to wait Stuart immediately put a
ban on meeting during the camp—until two days
later Joyce bumped into him on some stairs, burst
into tears and flung her arms round him. But it was
the last time they were to be so close for many
years. When the conference ended they went their
own ways, determined to live for Jesus Christ and
not to see each other.

By the time they met again, Joyce had recovered
from tuberculosis, which was diagnosed soon after
the camp, been through Bible training college in

Glasgow, met her husband again and remarried him after he had become a Christian.

Stuart's determination to live for Christ went with him from the camp, and immediately he entered the garage the following Monday he nailed his colours to the mast. Monty and the salesmen soon learnt that Stuart was a Christian; if his words weren't enough the never-ending trail of gospel leaflets and Bibles he left in glove compartments convinced them. Monty shrugged his burly shoulders, looked down at Stuart and growled: 'You don't mean it ? Not you ?' Then he laughed, a deep roar, and waved his fist at heaven, swearing and threatening God. Stuart was frightened God might flash down a streak of lightning on his partner, but nothing happened other than Monty stamping off laughing. The work-mates began to festoon the walls of the garage with pin-up pictures hacked from magazines and Stuart retaliated, pinning up articles from Christian magazines pointing to the reality of Christianity.

The Bible his mother had given him became a vital ingredient in his life. Stuart couldn't put it down, reading it at every opportunity including his fifteen-minute lunch break. So avid a reader was he that he had started the New Testament at Matthew and read through the Bible several times within a year or so. He began to read Christian books and magazines also, with the same intensity, learning of a conference on the Continent for young people who wanted to work for God.

For Stuart it was to be the beginning of a completely new phase of his life. The conference was to last a week with two months of practical evangelism afterwards, so he began to sell all his goods to raise the finance. The huge, spectacular American car, a Mercury Cougar, gold, red and black with over-sized wheels, was sold to a friend in the garage for the price he had paid for it; records, colour televi-sion—all were sold and with some of the money he bought his mother a new gas cooker. For the church he bought a range of coffee tables to service the coffee bar he had started himself for youngsters in the church basement a few weeks before. More money went in gifts to people in need and mission organisations.

When he handed his notice in at the garage Monty couldn't believe it. 'I knew you was religious but this is crazy,' he stormed. 'You've flipped your lid.'

Stuart arrived at the summer camp in a Bible Institute in Leuven, Belgium, excitement throbbing through his body. With eight hundred other young people present he couldn't get over the magnitude of the exercise. After a few days' training Stuart was selected to work in an Eastern European country—his first attempt at evangelism. The small team of four would take different Scripture leaflets and liter-ature and deliver them surreptitiously in letter-boxes, or where people would find them. The leaf-lets invited individuals to write for a correspon-dence course in their own language. But within a few days Stuart was to find out about the inside of Yugoslavia's prisons, something that, despite his vicious behaviour in Glasgow, he had always avoided before. He was discovered putting litera-ture into letter-boxes and arrested by the police.

He was taken to a cell and for two days saw no one except the guard who delivered a plate of food and drinks a couple of times a day. Taken from his cell on the third day he met two of his colleagues from the team—an American and a Swede—who had also been arrested. They thought they were being taken for questioning, and found themselves in a large room facing three officials seated behind a table. Two men and a woman, well dressed, motioned them to sit in chairs. They sat, the blue-and-grey short-sleeved-shirted guards, armed with pistols and truncheons, positioned round them. A large picture of President Tito glowered down from above the three interrogators.

The four young men said nothing, understanding very little as the officials chatted to police personnel. The only one of the quartet to speak was the American; he wanted to contact his embassy but the request was refused. After half an hour or so the four found their arms grabbed, and they were roughly dragged to their feet and frog-marched out of the building to a waiting police van. Thrust inside, the door was slammed and they heard the lock click. It was midday and the summer sun blazed onto the van, sending the temperature soaring; soon they were wringing wet with perspiration. Eventually they heard a driver and guard enter the vehicle and felt it move off, banging and jolting over what seemed cobbled streets.

When it stopped and the doors were opened they were pulled out to face the huge walls of a prison; iron gates broke the symmetry of the twenty-foot high walls, and inside they noticed a run-down garden before being marched into a medical room.

Their hair was shaved off as they stood naked, and they were given green fatigues. Individually they were locked in solitary confinement for several days.

Eventually they were reunited, placed in a large dormitory cell with up to sixty newly arrived prisoners; murderers, criminals, rapists and psychopaths. For once Stuart, who had spent most of his life wanting to be with the most violent and toughest elements in humanity, discovered he felt out of place and it wasn't just the language barrier. The four were allowed no phone calls, no visits and refused permission to write letters or even contact their embassy. All they discovered was that what they had considered to be a provisional questioning session, had in fact been a court hearing and they had been sentenced to forty days in prison.

Time dragged on. And all four were concerned that no one knew of their whereabouts. But a stray paragraph in a Yugoslavian newspaper mentioning the American's arrest had been picked up by an American who promptly contacted the embassy. When an embassy official asked to see his countryman he was allowed into the prison. He learned of the plight of the four and contacted the English and Swedish embassies. Despite pressure from all the embassies it was not until the forty-day sentence was up that the four were allowed out. Then they were pushed from the prison, told to leave the country and not return for five years.

The excitement for which Stuart had once beaten and crushed other people began to come to him now in more peaceful ways as he saw the powerful effects of the good news of Jesus Christ on others.

He was to make several trips into Eastern European countries, taking encouragement to Christians.

Stuart met and married Mary, an American, in 1982, after they had met in Turkey and spent time in America together on OM business. Now they have two children; Cameron aged three and Katherine aged twenty months. For Stuart life contains all the thrills he wants: he enjoys preaching about revival, is thrilled to talk of church growth and world mission and gets all the excitement he wants either talking to others about Jesus Christ or encouraging young Christians to do the same.

'Life is so full I don't know what to do next,' he enthuses. And the one-time Glasgow city boy still enjoys living in the city—except that now it is in Vienna, Austria, from where he directs much of the OM work in Europe. The tough guy from Scotland has Europe as his mission field.

II

Decision time

As England footballer Glenn Hoddle stood in the Church of the Nativity, Bethlehem, a day or so before England played Israel, he felt a strange emotion: he sensed that God was real.

It was a sensation that was to mean more to him than the match, days later, when his foot curled home England's goal. The soccer star had spoken to singer Cliff Richard weeks before and had read a Christian book by a BBC journalist, Gerald Williams. Those incidents, plus the visit to Bethlehem, were stepping-stones in his own journey to Christ.

Despite a glittering career with Tottenham Hotspur in England, and Monaco, in the French League, Glenn Hoddle knows that Christ, not soccer, has changed him. 'I didn't believe God could be there in the smelly atmosphere of a football changing-room—but he is,' he said.

A similar story has been repeated nine times in this book—although in nine different ways. A successful sailor with a weak heart; an intellectual

French woman; a Czechoslovakian army officer; a one-time male prostitute with AIDS; a depressive career woman; a travel-hungry Dutchman; a Muslim immigrant; a housewife, and a city-born man who lived by his fists—nine people, each very different, and each hunting for what they considered was the best that life could offer.

Individually some appeared to be successful in life; they reached the pinnacle of achievement through their own ability, initiative, or will-power. But somehow they didn't feel successful—they sensed another target, more important, calling them towards it. There was, for them, no sense of relief in reaching whatever they considered to be the top, finding excitement in study, drugs or sex. Nothing seemed to offer the ultimate. Instead they found only unsatisfied emotions, unrealised dreams and unattainable peace of mind.

Until they met Jesus! Then each person changed drastically. Few were recognisable after that incredible transformation. For some, becoming a Christian was a dramatic, instantaneous change of direction. For others, it was the result of patient searching, probing, questioning, and a sensitive response to an equally patient God.

Psychological and spiritual instability brought on by years of personal abuse hindered some from finding instant answers to life's problems. And in some cases—particularly Aids carrier Stefan Weiss, for instance—the results of their philandering and immorality will be trademarks they could carry for the rest of their lives.

As we spoke for many hours it became evident that even though each story was completely different there were some common threads: each person spoke of the feeling of despair and frustration that had come upon them early on in life when they had twinges of regret at their own actions, or sensed that there was something much more fundamental and important which they were missing.

I felt, often, that our paths had crossed; I had been there before. My own experience of a lifetime in journalism had introduced me to elements of the same despair and the sense of unfulfilled ambition. That feeling may have occurred to you as you have been reading. Human nature the world over doesn't change.

But the remarkable thing is that God didn't turn them away. And he promises a similar welcome to you, whatever your condition.

God specialises in the impossible: no one is too far down the road to miss his call, and none too successful not to need his love.

You might be able to freeze God out by ignoring him, or reject his claims on your life with a refusal to even consider his personal plea to you; but it will not affect his love for you at all.

The final chapter of this book spells out as clearly as it could be written how you can discover the joy, excitement, and complete radical change in outlook that the nine people brave enough to expose their lives for your benefit found.

Read on . . . try it!

12

The way ahead

I slunk from the tennis court having been heavily
defeated. My brother-in-law had triumphed again.
It wasn't defeat, however, that gave me the heavy,
leaden feeling inside: it was something far more
important than a game of tennis on the local council
courts.

I knew that on that Sunday evening in 1957 I
should have been in church. I had promised a girl-
friend to be there and instead, when she called for
me, had invented an excuse simply so that I could
escape what I knew would be a traumatic evening.
For something was gnawing away at my con-
science, telling me that I needed to think more
seriously about life and in particular about the
claims God was trying to make upon me.

Before that it seemed not to matter that much.
After all, God was someone who mattered only in
old age and when near death. I knew he existed and
even sensed that what I had heard about Jesus
Christ was true: he was the Son of God and did
demand personal commitment. My trauma ended

the following Sunday. I went to the church, didn't really need to listen to the message that the preacher gave, but afterwards knelt in submission to the claims of Christ.

There were no bright lights, no sudden feelings of elation or inward change; simply a quiet confidence in God that he would keep his side of the bargain. After all, he had promised in the Bible that anyone who came to him would be accepted and not turned away. That confidence was well-placed.

Centuries ago the second king of Israel, Solomon, spoke from experience when he said he had tried everything the world offered—wealth, fame and greatness. But instead of bringing happiness they merely brought him trouble and despair. They also seemed to cut him off from the God he claimed to serve. Depression set in as he realised that nothing that he could do seemed to make it any easier to keep in touch with God.

He described his own useless life in the Bible: 'Anything I wanted, I got. I did not deny myself any pleasure. I was proud of everything I had worked for, and all this was my reward.

'Then I thought about all that I had done and how hard I had worked doing it, and I realised that it didn't mean a thing. It was like chasing the wind—of no use at all.' (Ecclesiastes 2:10-11).

That futility and frustration is common in the hearts of many people today, restlessly searching for the answers when they can't even cope with the questions.

When you drive a car at night the lights have to be switched on and trusted as they illuminate what lies ahead; even so, they only expose the road for a certain distance. Sometimes bends restrict that vision to a short distance, at other times a long stretch of straight road will make the journey easier. To the driver it is enough, providing he or she is careful and prepared to drive within the limits of the view given to him.

That's how I see Christianity. It begins by switching on lights inside the mind and heart—contact with an outside agency that provides a new source of inspiration and illumination. For me it occurred at the age of seventeen when I recognised that despite all the energy and excesses of youth, despite the promise of a career in journalism, I needed something more in my life. I needed the foundation which I had seen in the lives of Christian friends—a stable relationship with God himself. I also had to recognise that because of the inability within me to do the right thing on every occasion, I had a lot of evil in my past that needed hiding if I were to stand in the presence of a clean, holy God. And I couldn't hide it. Even at seventeen I knew that everything was exposed to an all-seeing, all-knowing God.

I learnt, however, that Jesus Christ, God's Son, had agreed to be born as a man, live the perfect life, and then die on a cross simply so that by giving his life he could pay the price necessary for the forgiveness of my sin. He also miraculously rose from death after three days to guarantee eternal life for me.

The fact that Jesus did all that was one thing: but I had to make a decision—I needed to accept the fact that I was a sinner, needing God's forgiveness, and wanting his blueprint for my life. Once I had told God that I accepted his terms, his new life became mine.

At once the murky elements of my past were forgiven—in fact the Bible is careful to explain that God doesn't just forgive them, he forgets them completely. So completely that if I talk to him about them now he doesn't know what I am talking about. With a fresh start I was able to ask for help with my new life—and got it. Instantly on accepting Jesus Christ as my Saviour, God's Holy Spirit filled me with a new way of looking at life. I could talk to God in prayer and get guidance from the Bible, his Word as it has been handed down through generations.

But there were extra benefits also: I was part of a world-wide family—Christians, the children of God. That meant that in even the remotest parts of the world it was probable that there would be Christians who would become friends and accept me. True, we might have cultural differences and even varied views of our faith, but deep down the basic truths were unchanged—we all belonged to God through Jesus Christ.

I needed to keep contact with God and with other Christians, which meant a regular agreement to pray, read my Bible and attend a church where I could be part of a miniature demonstration of Christian love and concern.

Over the last thirty-two years it has worked! I haven't always been true to God, but he has been true to me. I have let him down on occasions; he has never let me down. I have discovered Christian friends are only human (they have found out the same about me) but when we are determined to please God and follow him, life is an exciting challenge.

Just as the people whose stories are reproduced in this book would admit, without Jesus Christ in their lives they could see no validity or purpose in it all. Life is, after all, to please God and to prepare us for an eternity with him.

Becoming a Christian is not as simple as it seems. It needs, for instance, your total acceptance that your life at this moment needs an outside influence, that many elements in your past need forgiveness and that neither of those things can be created within you.

'If we say that we have no sin, we deceive ourselves, and there is no truth in us. But if we confess our sins to God, he will keep his promise and do what is right: he will forgive us our sins and purify us from all our wrongdoing.' (1 John 1:8-9).

You then need to see what God wants to do for you. He created the world and man and woman, and then watched them slip and crash into wicked ways simply because he had given them the power to observe good and evil and make their own choices. You have that same power. Jesus died to bring you new life, but you can reject it and determine to go your own way. God will not bulldoze his way into your life. You need to do the inviting.

'For God loved the world so much that he gave his only Son, so that everyone who believes in him may not die but have eternal life. For God did not send his Son into the world to be its judge, but to be its saviour.' (John 3:16-17).

If you are prepared to invite Jesus into your life to forgive the past, give a new start, and unfold

God's better plan for your life—just ask him. In the silence of your own heart ask him to do it. That's the beginning of prayer.

Once done God will honour his side of the bargain. New life is yours. Now you will need to begin the long process of learning how to live all over again. Just as a child grows by taking milk and gradually being weaned on to solid food, until as a growing adult it can take all the calories required to conserve and power life, so you need to begin in a quiet, calm way, to adapt to your new life.

Start to read the Bible, using reading aids which can help with understanding and encouragement. Spend time daily praying to God—simply talking about your problems, thanking him for what he does for you, and sitting quietly allowing his thoughts to permeate your mind. Cultivate Christian friends and identify those with a mature faith who will be able to help you over some of the hurdles that await you in your new life.

The world-famous evangelist Billy Graham told me once: 'I have to tell people about Jesus Christ because he has done so much for me. I do not know how anyone can cope with the pressures and turmoil of life in the twentieth century without the peace and assurance that God alone gives.'

That, too, is my view, and the view of all those whose stories make up this book. God loves the world; he loves Europe; he loves you!

Love Europe

Breaking Free is more than just another book. It is a part of 'Love Europe', an exciting international effort to bring the good news of Jesus to contemporary Europeans. Christians from around the world will be involved throughout the 1990's, sharing their faith on the streets, in homes, schools, wherever they are welcomed through music, drama, literature, and especially personal friendship.

'Love Europe' is sponsored by Operation Mobilisation, who will be working alongside many other organisations and churches across the continent, including Eastern Europe. It was launched in July 1989 at a special 'Love Europe Congress' in Offenburg, West Germany, and is open to any committed Christian (over seventeen years) able to give two weeks or more of their time.

Reading *Breaking Free* may have challenged you personally to put your faith in Jesus Christ—or to

share that faith with others through 'Love Europe'.
In either case, please write for more information to:

Love Europe   or   Love Europe
Operation Mobilisation   Postfach 23
The Quinta   A-1037 Vienna
Western Rhyn   Austria
Oswestry
Shropshire SY10 7LT
England